The Gift of Contingency

American University Studies

Series V
Philosophy
Vol. 120

PETER LANG
New York • San Francisco • Bern
Frankfurt am Main • Paris • London

David Platt

The Gift of Contingency

PETER LANG
New York · San Francisco · Bern
Frankfurt am Main · Paris · London

Library of Congress Cataloging-in-Publication Data

Platt, David S.
 The gift of contingency / David S. Platt.
  p. cm. — (American university studies. Series V,
Philosophy ; vol. 120)
  Includes bibliographical references.
  1. Contingency (Philosophy) 2. God.
  3. Religion—Philosophy.   I. Title. II. Series.
BD595.P52   1991   123—dc20   91-18283
ISBN 0-8204-1543-X   CIP
ISSN 0739-6392

Die Deutsche Bibliothek-CIP-Einheitsaufnahme

Platt, David:
The gift of contingency / David S. Platt.—New York;
Berlin; Bern; Frankfurt/M.; Paris; Wien: Lang, 1991
 (American university studies : Ser. 5, Philosophy ;
Vol. 120)
 ISBN 0-8204-1543-X
NE: American university studies / 05

The paper in this book meets the guidelines for permanence and durability
of the Committee on Production Guidelines for Book Longevity of the
Council on Library Resources.

© Peter Lang Publishing, Inc., New York 1991

All rights reserved.
Reprint or reproduction, even partially, in all forms such as microfilm,
xerography, microfiche, microcard, offset strictly prohibited.

Printed in the United States of America.

ACKNOWLEDGEMENTS

I wish to thank Professors George Allan and Raymond Anderson for reading the manuscript and making many valuable suggestions. Any remaining deficiencies are my own. Wilson College offered assistance and support, specifically: the Paul Swain Havens Memorial Fund; Dean James Applegate for assistance; Susan Kump, Director of Computer Operations, for making the necessary font available and for help in formatting the manuscript. Christine Marra, Production Manager at Peter Lang, and Joshua Phillips, Production Assistant, willingly gave advice and assistance.

Most of all, appreciation must go to my wife, Helen, for support throughout the process. Her editorial assistance and her direct, no-nonsense criticism of philosophical obscurities in the manuscript have made this a much better book than it would have been otherwise. Again, thanks for just being there and being herself.

DEDICATION

To the memory of my parents,
JOE and EDITH

PREFACE

Historically, in the philosophical enterprise, contingency and necessity have been contrasted with each other, usually in terms unfavorable to contingency. Historically, certainty has been seen as a significant cognitive goal of both philosophy and religion.

In our more empirically oriented times contingent and probabilistic knowledge have achieved respectability and contingent knowledge is no longer "a poor relation" of necessary truths. Both types of truth are equally respectable.

Metaphysically, the historical "grand tradition" in philosophy has felt that ultimate contingency is unacceptable and unintelligible. The world must be grounded in a necessary principle of sufficient reason or a necessary divine being who is God.

A part of the Western theological tradition has thought not only that the contingent world must be grounded in a necessarily existent God but that *religiously* it is essential that God exist necessarily. It has been widely held that ultimate contingency is a curse rather than a gift.

This study will contend that ultimate contingency reigns, whether we approach it from a philosophical or religious context. Nature, man and God are all contingent and contingency is ultimately a gift rather than a curse.

The reader should be aware, if he is not already, that this study is an exercise involving philosophical speculation. Who knows whether contingency is ultimate or not? There is no experimental way to settle the issue. I am trying to make a plausible and coherent case for ultimate contingency.

CONTENTS

INTRODUCTION	WHY IS THERE ANYTHING RATHER THAN NOTHING?	1
CHAPTER I	WHAT IS IT TO BE CONTINGENT?	21
CHAPTER II	WHY ULTIMATE CONTINGENCY IS HATED AND FEARED	35
CHAPTER III	GIFT AND CAUSAL NECESSITY	53
CHAPTER IV	EXPERIENCE AS A GIFT	67
CHAPTER V	THE FELT DEFICIENCIES OF A CONTINGENT GOD	83
CHAPTER VI	THE ROLE OF REVELATION AND REASON	95
CHAPTER VII	DIVINE CONTINGENCY AS GIFT	119
CHAPTER VIII	THE ISSUE OF RELIGIOUS ADEQUACY	137
CHAPTER IX	CONTINGENT DIVINITY AND RELIGIOUS ADEQUACY	157
CHAPTER X	DIVINE UNIQUENESS	177

CHAPTER XI   DIVINE CONTINGENCY, SO WHAT? 187

CONCLUSION 201

BIBLIOGRAPHY 205

PERMISSIONS

The author gratefully acknowledges the following permissions to reprint:

From *Idea of the Holy,* 2nd ed., by Rudolph Otto (translated by John W. Harvey), 1950, by permission of Oxford University Press. All rights reserved.

From *Church Dogmatics*, Volume II, by Karl Barth (England: T&T Clark, Ltd.,1957). All rights reserved.

From *Basic Writings* by Martin Heidegger (edited by David Farrell Krell). Copyright 1977 by Harper & Row, Publishers, Inc., Copyright 1977 by David Farrell Krell. Reprinted by permission of HarperCollins Publishers.

From *Heidegger on Being and Acting,* by Reiner Schurmann (Bloomington: Indiana University Press, 1987). All rights reserved.

From *Science and the Modern World,* by Alfred North Whitehead. Reprinted with permission of Macmillan Publishing Company. Copyright 1925 by Macmillan Publishing Company, renewed 1953 by Evelyn Whitehead.

INTRODUCTION
WHY IS THERE ANYTHING RATHER THAN NOTHING?

The question indicated by the title is one of the old philosophical "warhorses" that has been with us for centuries. Not only is it an old philosophical issue, it is a question that could "sweep over" us at any time. If it emerges at all, it usually emerges while one is daydreaming or in a state of reverie when, as Wittgenstein said, the mind is out of gear and is idling. I remember as a child occasionally being struck with astonishment and wonder that I existed or that anything else did for that matter. I remember trying to carry out a thought experiment, shutting my eyes and trying to imagine what it would be like for there to be nothing at all anywhere, ever. The impossibility of the procedure became immediately apparent when I realized that I was there all the time, trying to carry out this thought experiment.

On a more sophisticated level, metaphysicians have worried for centuries about this issue while, through history, tough-minded empiricists have constantly ridiculed the question as unanswerable and meaningless. At times the issue has been very much in vogue and at other times, very much out of fashion. It has been a continuing part of the Continental European tradition and has generally been rejected with contempt by the Anglo-American empirical tradition.

Traditional classical metaphysics has attempted to answer the question in very specific ways. In theologically oriented positions, the obvious answer to the question is to speak of God's choice to create a world out of primal nothingness. In Aristotle's metaphysics recourse has been made to the Unmoved Mover that moves all else without moving itself. Later, what has been resorted to by various philosophers, most notably Leibniz, is an appeal to a principle of sufficient reason.

Leibniz makes a distinction between what he calls truths of reason and truths of fact. Truths of reason rest on the principle of contradiction in that the negation of a truth of reason is not only false but self-contradictory. Truths of reason are what are generally referred to now as logical truths, truths which cannot be denied without self-contradiction. Truths of fact, on the other hand, cannot be based on the principle of self-contradiction. It is a truth of fact that Harrisburg is the capital of Pennsylvania but if I deny that Harrisburg is the capital, the worst I can be accused of is falsehood. The denial, however, does not involve me in any kind of self-contradiction. Truths of fact are prime examples of contingent truths; they just happen to be true as a matter of fact and logic alone cannot determine their truth or falsehood.

From the viewpoint of rationalist metaphysics truths of fact cannot simply be allowed to "dangle loose" in their contingency. For classical rationalist metaphysicians like Leibniz it would be intolerable to have a contingent world that by luck, so to speak, just happened to be the case. Likewise, it would be intolerable to have truths of fact which just happened to be true. For Leibniz, truths of fact must be grounded in a rational principle and since they cannot be grounded on self-contradiction he grounded truths of fact on what he called the principle of sufficient reason. For any truth of fact such as "Harrisburg is the capital of Pennsylvania," there must be a sufficient reason for this to be true rather than false.

What applies to this example would apply to all truths about the actual world. For Leibniz, all such truths and the entire actual world itself would require a sufficient reason for being as they are. Thus, if we ask, "Why is there anything rather than nothing?" the answer Leibniz would give would be the same as to any other truth of fact. He would say there is sufficient reason for there being a world and for each of the things in the world. The sufficient reason in all cases, for Leibniz, rests on the free decree of God.

The sufficient reason for the world being as it is lies in the divine will which, according to Leibniz, chooses to bring into existence from all possible worlds the best of all possible worlds. It would be against the divine nature to choose anything less than the best. Leibniz's view concerning the best of all possible worlds was mercilessly satirized by Voltaire, who failed to note Leibniz's profound point that when we are considering the best of all possible worlds, we have to take account not of what is abstractly possible but what is concretely possible, what Leibniz calls compossible or possible together. Even if we grant the notion of compossibility, it is absurd to maintain that this is the best of all possible worlds because to maintain this it would follow that all changes could only be for the worse. To look at things this way would entail the stupidity of any actions.

Granted that Voltaire was wide of the mark in his satire, Leibniz's view is an extreme version of rationalism, seeking to ground all contingency in the divine will. One clear motive of his is to maintain the divine supremacy demanded by Christian orthodoxy. In addition, Leibniz seeks to reject ultimate contingency. We need not go further into the details of Leibniz's system but we should note in passing that Leibniz regarded the statement, "God exists" to be a truth of reason and disclosable by formal proof. From his rationalist perspective Leibniz argued that ultimately there are no truths of fact, for all such truths can be known by the divine mind a priori. The distinction between truths of reason and truths of fact is an epistemological distinction reflecting the limits of finite human knowledge. Since we are incapable of complete a priori insight into the real, we must rely on experience to uncover a large body of truths, and such truths are designated as truths of fact. Leibniz maintained that truths of fact are incapable of analysis by finite minds. At the human level there is brute contingency, but in the ultimate divine view of things there is only necessity.

Rationalism as represented by both Spinoza and Leibniz represents the most extreme philosophical attempt to eliminate ultimate contingency. Spinoza is the most extreme, regarding the world as a closed, deterministic, axiomatic system. Leibniz weakens Spinoza's extreme view by allowing the notion of possibility to appear as well as grounding contingency on the will of God to produce the best. Of course, Leibniz would maintain that it is part of the divine nature to produce perfection and that God's will is rationally necessary but free in that he is acting out of his own nature. Nevertheless, when rationalism introduces any kind of volitional element into things, a significant chink in the armor of rationalism appears. An axiom system cannot involve such things as will and choice without introducing an element of contingency. The only relations that an axiom system can tolerate are relations of logical entailment between axioms and theorems. Even though Spinoza's effort failed to produce the "tight" logical connections required, he at least saw that this was the position he must take. Leibniz, restricted by Christian orthodoxy, opted for an ultimate volitional choice by God to produce the best. To do so, however, is to introduce an element of contingency at the heart of his system, a consequence Leibniz attempts to avoid by saying that God acts out of the necessity of his own nature.

Whether we invoke God, the principle of sufficient reason or some other ultimate Ground, our main purpose is to reach a stopping point in inquiry. The mind must find a place to stop. Inquiry cannot go on endlessly. James referred to this overpowering demand for ultimate intelligibility as the sentiment of rationality. In the rationalist *thesis* of the Kantian antinomies, reason must reach a stopping point; inquiry cannot go on endlessly. Brute endless contingency is deemed unacceptable.

We are not supposed to go beyond this rationalist stopping point. It is deemed meaningless, if not impious, to wonder who made God, or what lies behind the principle of sufficient reason. To ask such a question at this point projects us into the unacceptable infinite of the Kantian *antithesis*. Nevertheless, an astute five-year old may well ask, "Who made God?" As Kant pointed out, while reason seems to demand a stopping point, reason can also always raise the question again of any stopping point proposed, "Why did x occur?" or "What is the basis of x?" The embarrassing point is that no reason one could give ever turns out to be sufficient; in the end, "anything at all," including God or the world as a whole, is a sheer gift of experience. It is unrequired and unnecessary, no matter how scientifically explicable it may be.

Experience makes any verbal or written answer invalid. Not only does experience drive us beyond any stopping point that the Kantian thesis may project but experience also destroys the infinite totality of the Kantian antithesis. All experience can say is that wherever we stop, we could proceed further because even an infinite *totality* can never be given in experience.

In appealing to the principle of sufficient reason or some other kind of ultimate Ground of Being, metaphysics draws a blank. It is difficult to see how any genuine *philosophical* enlightenment is derived by being told that God or a principle of sufficient reason explains the world. Philosophically, everything remains just as much a mystery as it did before. All that we accomplish by this gambit is to "close the road to inquiry." Many feel strongly that a cop-out has occurred when a rational Ground has been trotted out to explain the world.

When we turn from rationalist metaphysics to a purely religious perspective, however, the situation is radically altered. Here it makes sense and indeed is required to turn to God as an ultimate answer, but the "answer" here is to a religious question, often asked in existential anguish, not to the abstract question asked in metaphysics. In this context it is a question asked at the ontic level. People ask why their relatives had to die. No matter how painful it may be, the acceptable answer is often that it was the will of God. In this context, even if the answer is accepted, it does not furnish a startling new bit of information. One is not looking for a medical answer; one presumably already has that. Nor is one dealing with a metaphysical question of an abstract nature. Whether accepted or not as the will of God, the death of a close relative is something that can only be lived through with existential anguish and concern. In religious terms some kind of I-Thou encounter is called for. The cry of hurt and concern here is "light years" away from the abstract question as to why there is anything rather than nothing. God is an acceptable and natural answer to these questions because the answer called for here is a religious response of worship, not a demand for more information or rational grounding.

When we step back into the metaphysical context of inquiry, however, to reply that God or a principle of sufficient reason answers the question as to why there is anything rather than nothing closes the door of inquiry in an arbitrary way. It does not follow from this that we cannot invoke or use the concept of "God" in metaphysical inquiry at all. If the concept is coherently developed within a metaphysical system, its use is highly appropriate and legitimate. What is being objected to is its simple use in closing off the inquiry as to why there is anything rather than nothing. Whitehead, for example, introduces God quite sensibly as a crucial part of his metaphysical system, but even Whitehead speaks of God as the ultimate irrationality.[1] While God has significant metaphysical functions in Whitehead's system, God is not conceived as a rationalistic answer to the problem of contingency. Even if we reject the answer that traditional metaphysics has sought to provide, the question itself, as Heidegger has indicated, is still a significant and important one in spite of what tough-minded empiricists maintain. It is to this further inquiry that we must now turn.

The most obvious response to this question is to regard it as essentially meaningless. When a small child keeps asking, "Why?" beyond the context where it makes any sense to ask, we become impatient and angry. This response is partly because we are tired of the exercise, partly because we don't know how to answer the question and partly, I think, because we realize that the question can't be answered. The child does not phrase it the way metaphysicians do, but the end result is the same. The child may ask something like "Why is there yellow, daddy?" This question may come after a long series of questions and one can tell by the way it is asked that a simple causal answer will not suffice. If one tries this gambit by pointing out the conditions which produce the sensation of yellow, the child will push ahead until the mode of the question becomes, "Why is there x?" where what is being asked for is not another set of antecedent causal conditions but why there are x's at all, rather than there not being any x's. Though the child does not know it, she has pushed the inquiry into the realm of the classic philosophical problem, "Why is there anything rather than nothing?"

Most of us are inclined to say at this point that, though the child does not know it, the question is quite meaningless, at least meaningless in any reasonable scientific or empirical sense. Of course, one could trot out God or some kind of principle of sufficient reason but as we have already seen, the inquiring child will simply continue the inquiry. At this point one seems to have exhausted the issue. If the traditional metaphysical answer closes the task of inquiry and if empirically and scientifically the question makes no sense, once we have seen the logic of the issue, that should end all discussion. It seems that all that can be said at this level is that this is not a real question at all, for no answer could make any sense. If no answer can make any sense then no real question has been asked. We must just accept with "natural piety" the fact that a contingent world exists as it does.

Nevertheless, more needs to be said on the question. No matter how many times the issue is declared resolved by classical metaphysics or declared meaningless empirically, the question continues to reappear in philosophical discourse from time to time. Furthermore, the fact that astute children frequently go to the heart of the issue immediately should give us pause in rejecting the question altogether. It is also significant that Heidegger considered the question of why there is anything rather than nothing an issue of major importance, and he was quite familiar with the criticisms that we have examined.

I will suggest various ways of dealing with this very pecular question. The peculiarity may be that the question has to be lived through rather than answered. Perhaps accepting ultimate contingency in the world with "natural piety" is not as far off the mark as may at first appear. "Why is there anything rather than nothing?" gives expression to our basic wonder and surprise that anything exists at all. Experience, in all its wonderful and terrible manifestations, is a *gift*, not required and not necessary. As Sartre saw, existence of things in the world is "de trop," that is, too much. Nothing requires that there be anything whatsoever.

Even in the empirical domain, while we can ask why we received a gift from someone, in the true sense of giving, no reason is required; it just comes free gratis from one person to another. With the gift of experience, in general, no reason can be asked for. No matter how hard we try, the mystery of experience will always remain. As we wait and receive what Heidegger calls the disclosure of Being, experience will always produce something new for us to respond to.

Traditional metaphysics and rationally oriented theology, while willing to accept the contingency of the self and the world, have refused to accept ultimate contingency. They have always required a rational Ground or God to support the contingency of self and world. I want to argue that there is no ultimate rational Ground or principle of sufficient reason, as rationalists have required. Of course, I cannot prove that this is so, but I certainly want to argue for it. On the other hand, given the many intimations of divinity found in experience, it is quite possible that there is a God or that there are divine beings of some kind. If such be the case, I want to suggest that God too would be a gift to us, and thus contingent also, though not in the same way as contingent items in the world. If God exists, God does not make everything clear as rationalists contend. Mystery surrounds God as Otto and others have made quite clear. What could be more mysterious than the numinous quality of divinity? Indeed, mystery surrounds nature, man and God, in that none of these components need exist at all, but the most mysterious, surely, is God.   In describing the numinous, Otto says:

> ...I adopt a word coined from the Latin *numen*. *Omen* has given us 'ominous' and there is no reason why from *numen* we should not similarly form the word 'numinous.' I shall speak then, of a unique 'numinous' category of value and a definitely 'numinous' state of mind, which is always found wherever the category is applied. This mental state is perfectly *sui generis* and irreducible to any other; and therefore, like every absolute and elementary datum, while it admits of being discussed, it cannot be strictly defined.[2]

Otto goes on to speak of the numinous state as being one where we are overcome by a sense of what he calls our creature consciousness, a state of being overwhelmed by our own nothingness before an overpowering absolute of some kind. The numinous in art would be expressed by the aesthetically sublime. We think of the terms "awe" and "awful." The latter term has come to designate something bad or repulsive, but its root meaning refers to something that is apprehended as mysterious and pregnant with hidden meaning. Otto speaks of magic as being a dim, suppressed form of the numinous which becomes more explicit in religious worship.

The numinous is a significant aspect of our awareness of divinity but an aspect that has receded markedly from liberal forms of Christianity where the emphasis is more rational and intellectual with an orientation towards social issues.

Otto also speaks of the mysterium tremendum, experiences characterized not only by awe but as uncanny and weird. The world of ghost stories with their attendant dread reflect the mysterium tremendum. What do Otto's insights have to do with our concerns with divine contingency? The numinous and the mysterious are important aspects of religious experience, often suppressed or overlooked by overly intellectualist religious responses. It makes no sense to think of such experiences characterizing a God arrived at by pure reason, let alone a rationalist ground of Being. The numinous and the mysterious point to contingency if anything does. The sense of awe or dread characteristic of the numinous appears and disappears obeying no apparent laws of logical development. The sense of the numinous remains one of the many gifts of contingency, a surd and strange impingement on our everyday experiences.

The numinous as one aspect of divine disclosure points towards God as other than man and his categories of reason. The so-called wrath of God has been an aspect of divinity that has been hard to square with more humanistic approaches to God. Otto throws some light on this matter:

> 'Wrath' here is an 'ideogram' of a unique emotional moment in religious experience, a moment whose singularly *daunting* and awe-inspiring character must be gravely disturbing to those persons who will recognize nothing in the divine nature but goodness, gentleness, love, and a sort of confidential intimacy, in a word, only those aspects of God which turn towards the world of men.[3]

The more benign aspects of divinity are surely there, but Otto reminds us that God is "wholly other" as well.

Returning to the question of why there is anything rather than nothing, it does not require an answer, meaning by answer something that could be formulated and set down as definitive in rational discourse. What is required is that we "live through" the question raised by the existence of nature, man and God.

The reader may well respond that we are sinking into ineffable mysticism, and that this has no place in philosophy. There clearly is an element of mysticism but we are also trying to think through a difficult issue. All thinking requires discourse of some kind or other. Mysticism, while often accompanied by discourse, does not require it at all. Thinking is required to enter the dialogue of philosophy and, thus, requires discourse. Furthermore, thinking philosophically involves making epistemic claims that call for our attention. Mysticism does not necessarily do this; in fact, it frequently disdains to do it, though apologists for mysticism find it essential to epistemically support it. Even Zen Buddhists, who generally disdain linguistic discourse, cannot refrain from engaging in it, but their spiritual life does not require it.

Mystical feelings of wonderment in the face of the world and wonder at its existence are called for, independently of discourse, but thinking requires that we talk about this wonderment. The importance of the traditional question as to why there is anything rather than nothing points up the continued astonishment and awe at there being anything at all. It designates the awareness of the brute contingency of existence which we confront, the contingency of a gift.

If we try to answer the question in rationalistic terms, no satisfactory result in terms of further *understanding* ensues, as we have already seen. Taken in the context of religious worship and devotion, it can be seen as fully appropriate to speak of God as a resolution of the issue. This is because the question is now being dealt with in an *existential* manner rather than as an issue to be resolved in metaphysics or epistemology. What is made possible by uttering the question in a religious manner is for an I-Thou encounter between man and God to occur. In entertaining this question religiously, we lay ourselves open for impingement from the divine dimension of reality. We can only be ready to let something happen; the issue cannot be forced.

To bring in God, hoping that this will enlighten us metaphysically or epistemically, is useless. No further rational understanding is provided; the mystery of existence reappears again.

The question as to why there is anything rather than nothing is one way, among others, of opening us up for some kind of impingement of divinity on consciousness. The question is important to those who ask it seriously in the context of religious searching. I would suggest that it also may be existentially important to some outside the context of religious inquiry. To Heidegger it is important in a non-religious sense, not because it opens us to God, but because it may open us to Being, or because it opens us to the wonderment of there existing anything at all. In Heidegger it is an ontological rather than an ontic question. It calls for disclosure of some kind about our relation to Being. Such disclosure is lived through experientially. It is not a disclosure that is of any help in rational understanding.

For Heidegger, the question of why there is anything rather than nothing is induced by a primal wonder that there is anything at all. We are talking here more about a mood that can sweep over us rather than a question that is to be answered. As Heidegger says:

> Only because the nothing is manifest in the ground of *Dasein* can the total strangeness of beings overwhelm us. Only when the strangeness of beings oppresses us does it arise and evoke wonder. Only on the ground of wonder— the revelation of the nothing—does the 'Why?' loom before us.[4]

Heidegger is not dealing with the question in terms of traditional representative logical thought. Heidegger's "thinking" is not a thinking that explains but one that attends to what is disclosed as Reiner Schürmann has indicated.[5] Heidegger's response to our question is very much in line with the approach to contingency we will be taking in our study. As Schürmann says in his major work, Heidegger moves from principle to anarchy. *Arch*e and *telos* apply to things given for handling or producing. Overall, the terms apply to a universe that is grounded in some ultimate teleology involving a rational principle. Heidegger denies any such ground and, thus, moves to what could be called *anarchy*, not meaning by this a political doctrine but an absence of ultimate rational ground, in short, ultimate contingency.

Heidegger's later thought takes as a primitive notion the idea of Being as disclosure. Ultimately we have "coming to presence" which involves sheer presentation of beings to us, without ground, with no arche but just appearing, thus, anarchy. We function as beings in the world where things and events are disclosed to us. We can devise causal laws of these appearances and develop science, but ultimately we are faced with a world of brute contingency with no resolution to the question as to why there is anything rather than nothing. As Reiner Schürmann stated:

> To the traditional philosophical wonder, why *is there* being rather than nothing? Heidegger answers with the simple *there is*. Such an answer not only flies in the face of any quest for explanation, but it amounts to an option for the fortuitous, for the unstable.[6]

Man, the rational animal seeking ultimate rationality, seeks to transcend the givens of experience and find an ultimate ground or rationale to things. Heidegger, speaking of men as mortals in the fourfold, indicates that we must simply let the given be. This does not mean we do not pursue science and technology; it means that, as Heidegger puts it, "The world is without why." Heidegger's importance is that he restores the world to radical contingency. He rejects the traditional rationalist answer given to the question as to why there is anything rather than nothing. He also rejects the classical empiricist view of the question as meaningless. For Heidegger it is the important philosophical question of our time because it forces us to confront the issue of ultimate contingency. It is a profoundly empirical and existential question, though clearly not empirical in the sense of classical empiricism.

Looking again at the question of "Why" itself, if we engage in the thought experiment of trying to think of or imagine absolutely nothing, or the state of sheer nothingness, we get nowhere. If nothingness were a "state" at all, it would be something and hence not nothing. Trying to answer the question may be analogous to trying to solve Zen Buddhist *koans*, which are deliberately set up to "break" the rational mind-set and free it for direct disclosure in experience. One example of such a koan would be the question, "What is the sound of one hand clapping?" The more we think about it, the more it seems appropriate to treat the question, "Why is there anything rather than nothing?" as a kind of Zen koan. As a rational question demanding a rational answer, both are meaningless. But the intent in both may be to drive us towards an emotional feeling state where disclosure of some kind can occur. Clearly there is a strong mystical element here, but let us pursue its philosophical implications further.

When entertaining this question we might ask why "anyone" would create a world. Of course "God" is usually substituted for "anyone," but I would like to leave the question in this form for now. If the notion of creating a world makes sense at all, what rationale could be found for doing so? Why bother? I suppose that one possible response would be that "someone" needed a world to complete some kind of emptiness that was felt. Something like this is involved again in Whitehead's view that the world requires God and God requires the world, but for Whitehead neither was created by the other or created out of nothing. Of course, if "someone" creates the world because he or she needs it, then the question reverts to a standard metaphysical question where we can only stop when we reach God.

When we substitute "God" for "anyone" in the question, the traditional answer of Christian theology has been that God did not create the world because He needed something, but that God simply created the world out of a superfluity of His own goodness. God created the world by a volitional act, as a sheer gift; there was no necessity for Him to do so. The gift character of the world is, of course, very congenial to the line of inquiry we have taken all along.

But as we have seen already, the question can be pushed back further in a disturbing manner. Why would "anyone" appear to be present to create a world? Again the mind breaks and the koan-like character of the question emerges in full force. There is no explicable rationale for the appearance of "anyone" to perform this world creating function. Certainly the projection of an infinite series of "anyones" at this point would not help.

No matter what we might substitute for "anyone," there did not have to be the effort of appearing at all. Pure presentation of anything is uncalled for, a surd, a gift. On the other hand, sheer nothingness makes no conceptual sense, as we have seen, so we can only say there are x's of such and such a kind that happen to exist but need not have existed in any ultimate sense.

This returns us to the wonderment of Being, as such, which becomes such a matter of concern in the later Heidegger. Under Being would be included nature, man and God. Perhaps everything reduces in the end to the wonderment of Being, which in the end involves a process of presentations of beings in experience, a series of disclosures and hiddennesses.

Having reached this point we come upon an interesting aspect of the issue which has been pursued further in certain kinds of Oriental thought and which Heidegger pursues further, as well. Heidegger speaks of the "world without why" and suggests that it is in the nature of Being to open up for disclosure the beings of the world as a "play" of various forces.

The notion of the universe as sheer "play" is an interesting one. Not only does Heidegger entertain it, but it was a part of certain features of Buddhism and Hinduism much earlier. In these earlier forms it was maintained that the divine element in the universe "others" itself in the finite forms of life, to be entertained, so to speak, by the ensuing drama of events that work themselves out. For Heidegger, Being is available for disclosure to man in the multiform ways in which beings appear on the world stage. In the universe as "play" there is no principle of sufficient reason involved nor is there any kind of God-given or divine plan behind the unfolding of the universe, for Heidegger. No rational scheme is there to be uncovered. The world is sheer contingency, a play of forces, unfolding a multiplicity of cosmic dramas. I call it, rather unkindly, the world seen as soap opera.

A soap opera unfolds as a series of crises, one after another towards no ultimate end or culmination; there is always another development of plot tomorrow. Characters come and go and things and events continue indefinitely. It is also the case with soap operas that a great deal of time is spent in waiting for something to happen. This is to keep the viewer in suspense and also allows the writers to be somewhat laid back and lazy in developing a plot line. In the soap opera a simple play of forces occurs and various themes about human life get played out over and over again in various combinations and permutations.

When we think about it, particularly in the context of Buddhist play theology, soap opera is much like life. Things unfold and develop, much of it due to our planning, but much of it is a result of contingent accidental occurrences. In life, as in soap opera, a great deal of time is spent in waiting for things to happen. The great momentous events of life, both good and bad, are separated by large stretches of waiting for things to develop. Depending on what we are waiting for, the waiting is done with fear, dread, hope and various other anticipatory modes.

Of course the way most of us look at life and at soap opera, for that matter, is decidedly inauthentic both for Buddhism and for Heidegger. We are supposed to let go of our ego and our assertive will and be open to the disclosure of Being. We are to accept "the world without why" and remain open and receptive to the play of Being as it discloses itself to man. To be open and receptive in this way is successfully to "live through" the question as to why there is anything rather than nothing. The lesson of the question is to accept the gift of the world, all of it, the good and the bad. Nietzsche expressed this attitude by calling for us to accept openly the eternal return of everything with a joyous and creative attitude.

To do what is suggested here is preferable to trying to find some kind of principle of sufficient reason, which as we have seen is a snare and a delusion. However, from a religious perspective, there are some severe problems with seeing the world simply as "play," a cosmic drama or soap opera, serving as entertainment for whatever divine forces may appear. The main problem is ethical. If the divine component in the universe "others" itself in us in order to express its nature or be entertained, then there is something ethically obscene and indecent about the game. The extent of human suffering and tragedy down through the ages does not justify such games. Hegel said that in the development of Absolute Spirit in history, "Many a tender flower is crushed."

Various religious thinkers have found the notion of the universe as a theatre for "cosmic play" quite intriguing and acceptable. From certain Buddhist perspectives the self is an illusion, to be dispensed with. The veil of Maya hides from us our true situation. We cling fast to the ego and take it all so seriously. We should just be open to, and accept, the cosmic soap opera as a device in which the divine "others" itself in persons.

If we take this as an injunction to release ourselves from our technological modes of domination over the planet, the injunction is badly needed. But selfhood per se is a valued part of the gestalt of "being in the world." The self is no more or no less an illusion than the external world. If one is an illusion, so is the other. Each is real and each requires the other. There is also a plurality of selves to enter into I-Thou community.

The concept of the universe as divine "play" seems ethically offensive in light of the staggering tragedies involved in human existence. There is clearly a place for humor and perspective even in the divine, but the symbolism of God on the cross seems a more profound reading of the divine-human encounter than seeing it in terms of cosmic play. The moral dimension must be given its due.

In the end we are faced with ultimate mystery. If the universe is only a divine game, then the universe is profoundly bad and immoral. Human sacrifice on this scale is not justifiable ethically. Christianity and Islam tend to reject this view of the world though there are Christian theologians who see the concept of "play" as an aspect of divine grace.

I have presented the question of why there is anything rather than nothing as an introduction to our study of the gift of contingency. The question confronts us in the end with ultimate mystery. Neither science nor metaphysics can do anything with it. But its persistent reappearance in philosophical discourse suggests that it is a prime example of an issue to be "played out" in our experience.

NOTES

1. A. N. Whitehead, *Science and the Modern World* (New York: Mentor Books, 1963) p. 160.

2. Rudolf Otto, *The Idea of the Holy* (New York: Oxford University Press, 1958) pp. 6, 7.

3. *Ibid.*, p. 19.

4. Martin Heidegger, "What is Metaphysics?" in *Basic Writings* (New York: Harper and Row, 1977) p. 111.

5. Reiner Schürmann, *Heidegger on Being and Acting: From Principles to Anarchy* (Bloomington, IN: Indiana University Press, 1987) p. 50.

6. *Ibid.*, p. 130.

CHAPTER I
WHAT IS IT TO BE CONTINGENT?

Contingency is manifested most dramatically in the passing and ephemeral nature of events in time which come and go, each one never to return again. We say a word in anger, later wishing we could recall the moment in order to erase it but to no avail. A loved one disappears or grows up and moves away and we realize that past moments can never be brought back. We savor a moment of ecstacy and delight, wishing to hold on to it but realize that we cannot. We dream of lost opportunities, wishing we could go back and remake the past. We think of innocent childhood as being far rosier than it was. The element of risk in all that we undertake and the relentless passage of time are the earmarks of contingency that bear in on us constantly. As we age, we realize that our time is fleeting and limited and that the older we get the faster it goes. This is what contingency is all about; this is the atmosphere in which our own contingency is manifested. To speak of contingency as a gift or speak of it in value positive terms seems odd, to say the least, and yet, this will be a continuing theme of our study.

First we must speak more specifically about the term "contingency." There are several aspects which must be kept in mind. Consider any object and let us call it x. To say that x is contingent or that x exists contingently is to say that x is contingent upon y, where y has to be some other object or set of objects in the world which causes or brings about the existence of x.

When we say that x exists contingently or that x is contingent, we also mean that x exists at some time or other, but not at all times. Any object or collection of objects is caused to exist at particular times and will cease to exist at some future time.

In general we could speak of these two aspects of contingency by saying that the contingency of x means that when x exists, it exists for a finite time period within the context of a larger environment which brought it about.

When we think about it, we can see that contingency is not a particularly startling concept. Everything in the world and every collection of things in the world is contingent on a larger environment in which it resides and on which it is causally dependent. All contingent things exist for limited periods of time.

When we say that everything in the world is contingent we must note that there is an ambiguity in the term "world." We can use "world," as another term for the planet earth. This is probably its most frequent usage. In this case, to say that everything in the world and every collection of things in the world is contingent is to say that everything on the face of the earth and the earth itself came about because of something else, will exist awhile and then will cease to exist, a not very startling or exciting thesis, to be sure.

Things begin to get a bit more interesting when we speak of "world" in the second sense. Here the term covers much more than simply earth, though it includes that too. "World" can also mean everything that exists.[1] Here we get a catch-all term that is meant to be literally inclusive of all of reality. Now the thesis that everything and every collection of things in the world is contingent becomes much more complex and is highly debatable.

In this second usage of the term, God would have to be considered, in some sense, part of all that exists, though distinct from the earth and planetary system. That God, too, exists contingently has generally not been accepted by most persons who think about these matters. If we think back to our opening remarks about contingency, we can see that most persons do not think that God is causally dependent on anything, nor do they think that God exists only for a finite length of time. God, it is felt, must exist eternally. It is not generally thought that God exists within a larger environment, though most theists maintain that the earth and the solar system are distinct from God. Nevertheless, the earth and the solar system are generally thought to be radically dependent on God or, we might say, contingent on God's will. God, though not contingent Himself, would be the basis and foundation of everything else, all of which would ultimately be contingent on God's will. In addition to everything being contingent on God's will, it would also follow that any particular thing or collection of things would also be contingent on specific contingent causal factors to bring it about. This is the way most theologians conceive of God's relation to the world. Ultimately my existence is contingent on and dependent on the will of God but my existence was also dependent on my parents. In a sense I would be the joint result of the will of God and my parents. God would thus be conceived to act on the world but generally through contingent causal agents. Some would consider God's ability to produce miracles directly as an exception, but the rule would be that God's will is indirectly exercised through contingent causal agents.

Traditional Christian theology maintains that there is never any necessity that God create a world at all and that His doing so is a sheer act of creative goodwill on His part. Nevertheless, traditional Christian theology maintains that world, meaning everything but God, is radically contingent on the will of God for its existence. It is also generally held that if God's will did not constantly and continually manifest itself, everything else would immediately cease to exist.

Another option is to identify God with world, taking "world" to mean all of reality taken together. In this case we would have pantheism, a doctrine that appears in both Hinduism and Buddhism. God would be another term for reality taken as a whole. All that exists, taken together, would bring God to presence; the world would be the manifestation of God. The world would cease to be seen naturalistically, as only a collection of all things in the universe. All things in their togetherness would *be* God. Whether this whole would exist contingently or not is an interesting question.

Opposed to "contingent" is "necessary." If x is necessary, it is not simply that x happens to be the case but also that x must be the case. Mathematical truths are generally thought to be necessary. Two plus two does not just happen to be four. Given the meaning of numbers, two plus two must be four necessarily. The truths of mathematics are not held to be true contingently, based on what conditions happen to be actualized in the world. Another way of putting this is to say that two plus two is four does not only happen to be a feature of our actual world, but it must be a feature in all possible worlds.

It has stoutly been maintained in philosophical and theological tradition that God could not be God and exist contingently. If he cannot exist contingently then he must be thought to exist necessarily. This tradition would maintain that the statement, "God exists," is logically necessary or is necessarily true. The denial of a logical truth is not simply false, but self-contradictory. Thus, those who hold this position would agree with St. Anselm when he says, "Only the fool could say in his heart there is no God." If God exists necessarily or by definition, then to deny God is to do something more than utter a falsehood. To deny God's existence is to involve oneself in a self-contradiction as well.

There is a vast literature on the ontological status of God. Does he exist contingently or necessarily? Since we will be supporting divine contingency, we must see just what is maintained by those who argue for divine necessity. Those who support divine necessity say that the statement, "God exists," is logically necessary because God's existence is metaphysically necessary. What is meant is that God could not just happen to exist. All contingent objects including the world just happen to exist. Given different circumstances, other things or other worlds would exist instead of this one.

To say that God is metaphysically necessary is to say that God exists, no matter what, that His existence holds not only in the actual world but would hold in all possible worlds. This is what would be meant by saying that God exists eternally. Nothing contingent could be God, for what is contingent just happens to exist, is dependent on something else and also is unworthy of worship, for it might conceivably cease to exist altogether.

Let us return to the notion of world taken to be reality as a whole in the pantheistic sense. For pantheism, the divine is just reality taken in its totality. Is this totality necessary or contingent? Some have thought that world as totality exists necessarily, sheer nonexistence being unintelligible.

Sheer nothingness seems unintelligible, if for no other reason than the fact that I am here all the time trying to imagine what it would be like for there to be nothing whatsoever. Furthermore, pantheism would not accept total non-existence as meaningful because that would mean the denial of divinity too. Absolute non-being would be the elimination of pantheism as well as of everything else. A logical paradox occurs. If we accept a doctrine of pure non-being, the doctrine refutes itself, for it (the doctrine) has to be something in order to be considered.

If sheer nothingness is unintelligible and self-contradictory, then the opposite (namely that there is something) must be logically necessary. Thus, pantheism would seem to entail that the world not only exists but exists necessarily.[2] Spinoza drew the conclusion that the actual world is logically necessary. His pantheism is one of strict, hard, logical determinism of the most extreme kind. Not only does the world exist; it had to exist and could not be different in any way from what it is.

Regarding sheer nothingness as unintelligible, deterministic pantheism would have to hold that it is necessary that there be something (some world or other) but not necessarily our actual world. However, since Spinoza's deterministic pantheism does not admit the mode of possibility, what is not logically impossible is necessary. In the strict determinist view such as we find in Spinoza, everything that occurs in the world not only does in fact occur, but it must occur. Strict causal determinism is identified with the kind of strict logical necessity with which theorems follow from axioms in a formal system. For Spinoza, the world *is* a formal system, where everything that occurs had to occur.

In such a view it would be meaningless to speak of possibilities which might have occurred but didn't or possibilities to come. *We* think of possibilities unrealized and possibilites to come because we are finite and we are ignorant of the iron-clad necessities that unfold as they must unfold. The situation is analogous to the one where we are trying to prove a theorem in a mathematical system. In the process of the proof we may think that theorem three follows from a given set of axioms or possibly that its negation will follow. We don't know which. But within the formal system itself, either theorem three or the negation of theorem three follows with logical necessity, whether we are able to prove it or not. Furthermore, *we* entertain two possibilities before proof is carried out. Either theorem three or the negation of theorem three will be proved, but not both. If theorem three indeed follows from the axioms, then the negation of theorem three is not only false but self-contradictory. If the negation of theorem three follows from the axioms, then theorem three is not only false but self-contradictory as well. Readers who have done indirect proof in mathematics will be familiar with the procedure involved here.

In Spinoza's world of extreme determinism, *we* may not know whether it will rain in Fayetteville tomorrow and *we* say that it possibly will or possibly won't. In Spinoza's world, it will either rain or not rain in Fayetteville tomorrow but we don't know which. However, if rain is destined in fact to occur, to assert that it will not rain in Fayetteville tomorrow is not only false but self-contradictory as well. If rain is destined not to occur in Fayetteville tomorrow, to assert that it will is not only false but self-contradictory.

In the world of pantheistic determinism what is actual is also logically necessary and what is not actual is not only false but is logically impossible or self-contradictory as well. These are the only two alternatives, necessity or logical impossiblity. Since what is actual is clearly not logically impossible, what is actual is also logically necessary for Spinoza. The notion of the possible but not actual is meaningless in such a system.

Pantheistic determinism sees itself as a complete, comprehensive closed system with no loose ends. The actual world is also the necessary world but the fly in the ointment remains. Where does the *actual* come from? Reason or logic alone cannot provide it. Obviously the actual comes from experience and what is given in experience is manifested contingently; experience could be otherwise than it is. What is actual arises only out of a range of possibilities. All actions that we undertake occur in a context of possibilities, only some of which we wish to actualize. Experience constitutes the downfall of pantheistic determinism as well as of any strict or hard determinism. Experience makes it implausible to see reality as a closed system modeled after an axiomatic mathematical system.

Leibniz was forced out of strict determinism by resort to God's volitional choice of the best. Spinoza's attempt to hold on to strict determinism forces him to say that the only thing that restricts existence is self-contradiction. Since there are only two options in Spinoza (necessity or contradiction), he is forced into the very odd position of saying that if anything is logically possible it necessarily exists or, to put it another way, the only thing that can prevent the existence of something is if it is a self-contradiction such as a round square. A thing necessarily exists if no cause or reason can be found which prevents its existence.

Given Spinoza's view we would seem to be driven into the absurdity of saying that blue grasshoppers with seven eyes exist because, though odd, there is nothing self-contradictory about such creatures. Spinoza could respond, however, that one must be more specific. He would argue that given the world we have, with all its causal laws and its logical necessity, blue grasshoppers with seven eyes would be inconsistent with such a world and the biological laws that describe it, though the concept of such grasshoppers taken by itself does not seem to be self-contradictory.

Nevertheless, Spinoza's view is very odd and flies directly in the face of experience. Experience consists of a temporal unfolding but there is no place for time in an axiomatic system. It may take us some time to prove a given theorem from a set of axioms but the theorem either follows logically from the axioms or it does not, and such implication is completely non-temporal. Experience is temporal throughout but there is really no place for time or any intelligible account of time in pantheistic determinism.

We said awhile back that deterministic pantheism would have to maintain, as a minimum, that something (some world or other) must exist because sheer nothingness was assumed to be unintelligible. Looking at the matter further, it is far from self evident that sheer nothingness is completely unintelligible. While we may not be able to grasp sheer nothingness in an intelligible concept, it is imaginable and is existentially quite significant. The existential concepts of dread and anxiety give testimony to the awareness of sheer non-being which can come over us. We are aware primarily of our own possible non-being; we are the mortals of Heidegger's fourfold. Awareness of death can also bring the angst of sheer non-being to presence in our consciousness. We can go further, not so much in terms of dread of sheer nothingness but, rather, *wonder* at there being anything at all. In the last analysis it is quite odd that anything whatsoever exists. No principles of logic or reason require that any actuality manifest itself. That anything is actual is a fragile contingent gift of experience, as we shall see. If it weren't for the sheer gift of actuality manifested in experience, the whole dialectic of pantheistic determinism could never have been started.

Regarding the world as logically necessary leads to irresolvable paradox, and Spinoza assumes that what there is has to be and could not have possibly been different in any way. If you start with logical necessity you end with it and you end with paradox, no freedom, no choice, no possibility. The pantheist can identify the world with God if he wishes, but the world so identified is our actual contingent world and, thus, any consistent pantheism would have to regard divinity as contingent too. Furthermore, given the actual world, there would be all kinds of possible worlds which might have been but are not. Thus, pantheism would seem to entail divine contingency since God is identical with the actual world.

Most *religious* pantheists would not describe the world in terms of necessity or contingency. The question is left open. This indicates that necessity and contingency are of little or no importance when it comes down to the actual life of worship, but are primarily of theological and philosophical interest.

The religious pantheism most familiar to us is found in Hinduism and it is a tradition with a very long history. Hinduism is a diversity of complex doctrines and observances, just as is Christianity. Nevertheless, running through Hinduism is a monistic strain, often referred to as Brahman, of which everything in the world is a part, hence, pantheism. Often the empirical world of diversity, plurality and change is contrasted with the static eternality of Brahman. Often the world of plurality and change characteristic of contingency is declared an illusion, a veil of maya behind which stands the unchangeable world of Brahman.

As in the Christian West, Hinduism tends to declare the changeless and eternal to be what is ultimately real and what is changing to be illusory. As in certain strains of Christian thought, contingency gets downgraded in status from the eternal, but religious pantheism does not put the heavy emphasis on necessity or logical ground that Western rationalism does.

Dissatisfaction and concern with the purely contingent remain. Contingency and change embedded behind the veil of maya are to be overcome by removing the veil through meditation practices revealing the stable and eternal oneness of the universe.

Not all forms of Hindu pantheism brand the changing world as total illusion. For some, Brahman is *in* as well as transcending the empirical world. The world of contingency and change, though referred to as maya, is often seen as a divine play or game in which Brahman or the One "others" itself. Hinduism sometimes speaks of the world as divine play or sport of magical illusion, partly real and partly not real. Enlightenment, of course, consists in seeing the play for what it is and we are encouraged not to take it too seriously. In any case, religious pantheism of whatever form seems more congruent with contingency than the logical necessity one sees in the deterministic pantheists.

Let us turn to panentheism. Panentheism is the doctrine that God includes the world (everything else but God) as a part of Himself, but there is much more to God than just the world. In such a view God could be necessary, but contain our world or another as a contingent part of Himself. All that is required is that God have some world or other.

Whitehead's is probably the most respected and original panentheistic view in the West. Though there is some ambiguity about God's ontological status in Whitehead, the tendency is to see God as contingent. Whitehead does not seem to come out unambiguously for either divine necessity or contingency. In a famous and frequently quoted passage he seems to opt for divine contingency. Citing God as a ground for limiting what occurs in the world, Whitehead goes on to say:

> This attribute provides the limitation for which no reason can be given: for all reason flows from it. God is the ultimate limitation, and His existence is the ultimate irrationality. For no reason can be given for just that limitation which it stands in His nature to impose.[3]

On the other hand, in the same work Whitehead says:

> Faith in reason is the trust that the ultimate natures of things lie together in a harmony which excludes mere arbitrariness. It is the faith that at the base of things we shall not find mere arbitrary mystery.⁴

Whitehead goes on to say that such faith lies at the base of science.

In the latter quotation Whitehead sounds more like a traditional rationalist looking for a rational ground. His admiration of Plato and his attitude of regarding all philosophy as a footnote to Plato is well known. It is interesting to note that this attitude towards reason is based on *faith* and, as Whitehead himself says, is not justified by any kind of induction. Today, rather than faith, we might speak of our reliance on reason as a normative stipulation for science, a kind of Kantian regulative idea.

The ambiguities in Whitehead on this point are well brought out in an article by William A. Christian, "The Concept of God as a Derivative Notion."⁵ The point to keep in mind is that a consistent panentheistic position can be developed with contingency seen as ultimate.

Charles Hartshorne, who has done the pioneering work in Whiteheadean process theology, sees consistent panentheism as requiring God as a necessary being. Needless to say, his position is opposed to the one taken in this study. His position is familiar to many and has been repeated in his books. I do not propose to restate his position or my response to it in detail at this point. Discussion of the issue can be found elsewhere.⁶ Hartshorne makes an impressive case but I think it ultimately collapses on the shoals of experience. The main rationale for believing in God involves divine disclosures of various kinds in experience, and experiential disclosure is contingent, not necessary. The rest of our study will develop this theme.

Whether one deals with theism, pantheism or panentheism, plausible positions can be developed in all three in which God is seen as contingent.

Returning to pantheism, the world or all actual reality which exists contingently is also regarded as divine. This is a plausible view, but what it amounts to religiously is seeing the world in a certain light, namely as impregnated by divinity. Change the focus slightly and you have the world of metaphysical naturalism. Given the purely contingent world and nothing else, doesn't the specter of sheer nothingness at all raise its head again? As contingent, the world could possibly cease to be. But we have already seen that the concept of sheer nothingness seems unintelligible.

Yet *dread* and anxiety concerning nothingness make sense and frequently occur. One wonder remains when all is said and done, namely that anything whatsoever exists at all.

Many philosophers, including Heidegger, speak of nothingness and of how we live against a background of non-being. Nihilism is equated with nothingness. There are a host of ambiguities in such talk. Frequently, what is of concern is our own possible extinction, such as we find in Heidegger's talk of being towards death. As for nihilism, concern about it generally centers around the absence of objective moral or cognitive standards, not sheer non-being.

While a doctrine of sheer non-being is not intelligible and cannot even be formulated consistently, I do want to stress *astonishment* that there is anything at all whatsoever. Others have thought that the notion of there being nothing whatsoever is intelligible even if we cannot imagine it. The issue of nothingness remains one of the most perplexing issues in philosophy with many ramifications.

Returning to the Christian tradition we can say that, taking "world" to be everything other than God, it has generally been maintained that the existence of the world is contingent. It need not have existed, but does in fact exist, contingent on the will of God. In addition, what has generally also been maintained is that the existence of God is necessary, not contingent. That is to say, God does not simply happen to exist, He must exist.

If your head is spinning at this point, we can sum up our results simply. Leaving God and mathematics aside, we can say that contingency reigns, in that everything that exists or any collection of things that exists, exists contingently. About this point there is rather general agreement. What is usually rejected strongly is the idea that God could exist contingently. Why such rejection is so insisted upon will be dealt with in the next chapter.

NOTES

1. Given developments in modern physics, there are those who deny that speaking of the universe as a whole or given totality makes sense. For our purposes we can leave this issue aside.

2. What is ignored here is that it is only necessary that there be something or other, some indeterminate x. It does not follow that this *actual* world has to exist, but only *some world* or other.

3. Alfred North Whitehead, *Science and the Modern World* (New York: Mentor Books, 1963) p. 160.

4. *Ibid.*, p. 24.

5. William A. Christian, "The Concept of God as a Derivative Notion" in *Process and Divinity* (LaSalle, IL: Open Court Publishing Company, 1964) pp. 181–203.

6. See Appendix to Chapter VII and my *Intimations of Divinity* (New York: Peter Lang Publishing Company, 1989) Chapters 1 and 2.

CHAPTER II
WHY ULTIMATE CONTINGENCY IS HATED AND FEARED

Why has necessity been assumed as ultimately preferable to contingency? The philosophical rationale can be found in Aristotle's contention that everything that moves must be moved by another and that the series cannot go back forever but must be grounded in a First or ultimate Prime Mover. Generally the mainstream of the philosophical tradition has thought that to accept ultimate contingency is to accept philosophical unintelligibility and it has been felt that the task of philosophy has not been completed until ultimate intelligibility has been shown.

Down through history, most philosophers have felt that an infinite series of reasons without beginning is unacceptable. Some thought that the temporal series could not go back endlessly but must have a first temporal mover. But even if an endless temporal series of becomings were accepted, it has been felt that the entire series needed to be grounded in a rational and logical first principle. Even if time had no beginning everything had to be grounded in a logically ultimate principle of sufficient reason.

Science presents us with a degree of intelligibility, perhaps the only intelligibility we are likely to get, but science is not worried about an ultimate ground or reason and presumably has no need of one. It is true that science looks for laws of greater and greater generality or searches for one ultimate principle of physical explanation, but this search can be adequately interpreted as a *normative* requirement of scientific inquiry. A norm directing us to look for more inclusive covering laws is quite different from a metaphysical claim that there is an ultimate rational principle or Being behind the world.

The metaphysical urge behind the search for a rational ground is more adequately explained by James as a sentiment of rationality. He sees the ground of Being as fulfilling a psychological need rather than answering to a metaphysical necessity. Interpreting the ground of Being in empirical terms, James sees the sentiment of rationality as a "feeling of the sufficiency of the present moment, of its absoluteness, this absence of all need to explain it, account for it, or justify it."[1] He interprets it as our pleasure in finding or bringing order out of chaos. Our minds are set at rest when we can reduce to the familiar what is alien and unfamiliar to us. This is what James calls rationality. The sentiment of rationality refers to a psychological need whereas metaphysical rationality refers to something which is regarded as basic to the universe itself.

We should add here that metaphysical rationality is a rather narrowly felt esoteric need of rationalist minded philosophers, certainly not a widely felt human need like the desire for God. But as a need felt by such philosophers, it is assumed that a necessary ground is much preferable to ultimate contingency.

While science can indeed bring some order out of chaos, its accomplishments are limited, not ultimate. Furthermore, as science advances it tends to raise more questions than it answers and continues to open up a world to us that becomes vastly more mysterious than the world as seen by nineteenth century mechanists.

While we need not belittle the desire to bring order out of chaos, it would seem increasingly that contingency reigns as we peer ever more deeply into the empirical universe. The search for a rational ground seems to reflect an esoteric psychological need masked as a logical requirement.

Before we leave this aspect of the matter we need to ask ourselves whether resorting to a principle of sufficient reason or rational ground really does make things more intelligible. Leaving aside the question of a psychological sentiment of rationality, what is being asked for logically when the demand for ultimate intelligibility is being made?

There are various kinds of intelligibility which we rely on that fall short of ultimate intelligibility. In everyday life we try to make intelligent sense out of all kinds of confusing situations. A detective solves a murder case, a mechanic finds out what is wrong with our cars or a new cure is found for a perplexing disease. Here intelligibility seems to fall under what Dewey referred to as rational inquiry. Faced with a problem that pure instinct and habit cannot solve, we deal with it by rational and empirical inquiry until the solution is found.

Science is a more subtle and complex inquiry than occurs in everyday life, but Dewey's model of intelligent inquiry continues to play a role in scientific contexts. Scientific inquiry is often much more theoretical than Dewey's more pragmatic approach would indicate, but in both everyday life and science only a relative degree of intelligibility is desired or asked for. Clearly such intelligibility is achievable. When we have achieved various finite answers to our problems, inquiry ceases at that point and we turn to other emerging problems.

What remains a mystery logically is how the simple reliance on God or a principle of sufficient reason provides ultimate intelligibility. It is widely assumed that to make such a move provides what is wanted, but even when the move is made, the mystery of the world remains as it was before. By invoking God or an ultimate principle of explanation, we have given another mysterious name to the proposed solution. God or the principle stares us in the face, and though we shouldn't do so, we can go on and ask, "Why God?" or "Why an ultimate principle?" I have never been able to see why when this traditional stopping point has been reached, things suddenly become *metaphysically* clear. That God or ground might bring the mind to rest in a *sentiment* of rationality is understandable, but that is something quite different from clearing up matters logically.

It may seem like beating a dead horse to press the issue of ultimate intelligibility. Most contemporary philosophers are not rationalists. Nevertheless, while rationalism may be out of current philosophical style, what is fashionably current does not determine philosophical worth. Many philosophers and theologians feel that this kind of metaphysical necessity is a requirement. When all is said and done, it would appear that all such attempts to achieve rational necessity fail, and they fail because of the open-ended nature of experience. Experience continues to be multifaceted, ambiguous and perplexing and its continuance destroys any hope of ultimate rational completion. The contingent givens of experience always break any complete synthesis apart and this is papered over by falling back on God or an ultimate principle. Also, the fact that something occurs rather than nothing at all remains a surprising mystery which cannot be successfully papered over by an appeal to ultimacy which remains just as mysterious as anything else. Philosophically, the demand for necessity and ground fails.

In traditional Western philosophy the assumption has been made that the world is ultimately intelligible and, as stated previously, that the task of philosophy is to discover this ultimate intelligibility. At the most extreme, ultimate intelligibility has seen the universe as being analogous to a mathematical deductive system. Spinoza is the standard representative of this view. Usually, however, the demand for ultimate intelligibility has settled for much less. Traditional Thomistic thought, for example, sees the universe as ultimately intelligible in possessing a basic Ground, this Ground being God. Other thinkers have spoken of ultimate Ground or a Principle of Sufficient Reason. Given a Ground, it was not regarded as essential to see the ties within the empirical world as ones of deductive necessity. Contingency could reign in the empirical world, but it all had to be ultimately grounded in God.

This traditional picture of the task of philosophy has been seriously undermined by certain crucial factors. One is the exploding bounds of human knowledge and the fragmentation of cognitive disciplines into more and more highly technical specialties. Also as we gain more human knowledege the area of mystery deepens and the elusive goal of ultimate intelligibility fades further into the background. It was one thing to claim such intelligibility when Aristotle could take all knowledge as his province, but something else again to make such a claim today.

The controversy over the role of philosophy has become sharper as time goes by. Leaving aside the positivist revolt, philosophers from various schools of thought increasingly deny that the task of philosophy is to uncover ultimate intelligibility. Foundationalism in epistemology seems outdated, and a similar attempt to find an ultimate foundation in metaphysics seems outdated too.

Styles in philosophy come and go, to be sure. Nevertheless, the decline in the search for ultimate intelligibility is of major significance for it reflects the growing awareness that the more knowledge we gain, the more mysterious and impenetrable the world becomes. In the past it was widely assumed that given time we would close in on reality as a whole and capture it eventually in our conceptual nets. We know now that this is an illusion. This does not denegrate the knowledge we have attained or will yet obtain, and such knowledge that we gain of the contingent world is not threatened by the absence of ultimate intelligibility.

While the demand for necessary ground seems out of place as a philosophical demand, this urge takes on quite a different aspect when it is seen as fulfilling a religious rather than a purely philosophical quest. In this context, at least in the West, "God" becomes the operative term rather than "Ground." The search for God is radically different from the search for ground, though the two have generally been conflated together in the tradition. It is frequently assumed that once we have established a rational ground we can translate this into religious terms, substituting God for ground.

James's sentiment of rationality is much closer to the demands of the religious consciousness than it is to the demands of rationalistic philosophy. We hope for some kind of assurance that the world makes some kind of sense or at least the religious consciousness wants some psychological assurance that life is worthwhile and the religious quest meaningful.

Ultimate contingency is looked on with great uneasiness by many theologians, particularly in the Catholic-Thomist tradition, as well as by a large number of philosophers because what is contingent is what is insecure and ephemeral and all of us tend to be uneasy about insecure ephemeral things. In the passage of time all things, events and persons come into existence and with the inexorable unfolding of time all things, events and persons are destroyed or pass away. We have attempted in vain to hold on to what we like, to arrest the flow of time by seeking permanence and stability for what we value. We erect monuments of various kinds to preserve and hold on to our dear ones and what they represent. In the face of the corrosive passage of time, we have embraced various doctrines of immortality. With all of our attempts, time continues to devour, not only individuals, but great civilizations as well.

Temporal passage is the mark of the contingent per se. In our philosophies and religions, we have searched for certainty, something that will ensure stability and permanence against the flux of change. In the Judeo-Christian West, God has generally been seen as this certain mark of permanence in a sea of change. Saint Augustine set the tone of Christian theology in the early church by his belief that God is completely outside of time and thus removed from the dangers of temporal contingency. In the realm of the certain and necessary, psychological and religious security is to be found. In the East, union with the divine in a state of Nirvana was sought as relief from the contingent changes of everyday life.

Religion has generally been seen as the main refuge from the giddy changes of contingency. We feel a profound need to achieve permanence. In our recorded history men have found the changing world of contingency frightening and have sought refuge from the world by searching for permanence and stability. Ironically, fear of the contingent is most dramatically expressed by our contemporary, Jean Paul Sartre, an atheist.[2] In his technical, philosophical writings and in his plays and novels, Sartre again and again presents the contingent world as metaphysically absurd because it is not grounded in God or supported by any kind of sufficient reason. Ironically, he agrees with traditional theologians who also would see the contingent world as metaphysically absurd unless it were grounded in God. But for Sartre, since there is no God, the world *is* metaphysically absurd and, with no God, "everything is permitted." For Sartre, the contingent world is "*de trop*," too much, and the "viscous stickiness" of contingent givens induces nausea in him. The world as "being-in-itself" is recoiled from in horror.

Seldom in philosophy or in literature has the disgust and fear of contingency been so dramatically expressed. One finds a similar fear and disgust with the empirical world of contingency in the writings of Augustine. From Augustine to Sartre, the fear of contingency has been expressed time and again, but not in as stark and dramatic terms as Sartre used.

The language of absurdity expresses basically a religious fear that the world alone has no ultimate goal or rationality in itself, whether this fear is expressed by Augustine or Sartre. There is a widespread fear of brute contingency. Sartre as well as many religious thinkers finds the contingent empirical world nauseous; nothing can be of real value if it ultimately passes away in the grinding maw of contingency. The main difference between Sartre and the classical religious tradition is that Sartre does not believe that there is a God. Sartre believes that "Man is a useless passion" who constantly tries to take the place of God but without success. The tragedy of man is that there is no God and he is thrown back on his "dreadful freedom" in utter frustration. Sartre is an atheist, to be sure, but he is not a happy one. The theologian can fall back on God; Sartre has no recourse but nausea and "authentic decision" in the face of metaphysical absurdity.

The world can be regarded as metaphysically absurd only by those who insist on God as a necessary Ground for the contingency of the world and fail to find such a God. If we accept experience in all its contingency or try to make sense of it piecemeal by means of science, then the question of metaphysical absurdity is never raised. Empirical naturalists do not call the world absurd; only disappointed existentialists like Sartre talk this way. Those who accept all of experience in its contingency, including the divine component as contingent, do not find the world absurd either. Zen Buddhists come the closest to fitting this description. Metaphysical absurdity can only be the product of disappointed rationalists; they insist that ultimate contingency is intolerable and go on to demand a grounding of contingency in a necessary God or a principle of sufficient reason but never find it.

As we shall see, religious worship and relation to the divine involve aspects of much more importance than finding refuge from ultimate contingency in a static and unchanging reality. We seek a refuge in God from the empirical absurdities and stupidities of everyday life, but this is a different matter than seeking relief from metaphysical absurdity. It is in seeking relief from metaphysical absurdities that the Greek influence, particularly of Plato, has had unfortunate implications for Christianity. The emphasis on the static and unchanging nature of the Forms as ultimately real, and on the world of becoming and change as illusory, when brought into Christianity, led to the view that God, being most real of all, must be static, unchanging and logically necessary. The ideas of an unchanging God are foreign to the Bible and to early Christianity. Christianity should not have to stand or fall on whether or not God is a necessary Ground of contingency.

As for empirical absurdities, these are aspects of the world that cause us concern and may help direct us towards religion. Empirical absurdities involve the luck and chance we spoke of earlier that are a part of contingent existence in the world. Empirically, the term "absurd" refers to events that affect our lives negatively—events which by a slightly different throw of the dice would have turned out differently. A particularly striking example of this empirical absurdity can be seen in the story line of the movie, *The Treasure of Sierra Madre*.

In the story, after mining gold in Mexico under severe and harrowing conditions, two surviving prospectors lose all their gold by a chance occurrence at the end of the picture. By an odd set of circumstances all the gold dust they gathered is blown back to the mountains from where they had so laboriously unearthed it. All their struggle and suffering was of no avail in the end against the "whims of fortune." Empirical absurdities occur as surprising negative gifts of misfortune. Each of us can think of our own examples of empirical absurdity, some trivial and funny and some terribly tragic. Sartre also gives examples of empirical absurdity, hoping in this way to lend support to metaphysical absurdity. The two types of absurdity are different, however. Empirical absurdities do not entail metaphysical absurdity.

When we speak of things and events as absurd in the ordinary sense, we are referring to empirical absurdity. Here all we mean is that some particular phenomenon doesn't make sense or "hang together" in a sensible or rational manner. Something happens that, given all we know, should not have happened. The term is also generally applied to value negative events that affect us and others badly. Faced with a traffic jam two miles long and no cops anywhere in sight, a driver may explode, saying that this situation "is unreal." Another example would be relief supplies which, given to a starving country, remain on the dock to rot because no provision has been made for distribution of the food. Empirically the term, "absurd," can be applied to unexpected happenings that are value positive but generally the term is applied to value negative events only. The term itself is emotively negative in character. The contrasting term, which descriptively is very similar, but is emotively positive, is the term, "gift," which we will look at shortly.

Empirical absurdities occur no matter what metaphysical or religious view you hold about the nature of the universe. Such absurdities have little to do with metaphysical absurdity, one way or the other. By trying to use empirical absurdities as evidence of metaphysical absurdity, Sartre and other writers confuse the issue for the latter does not follow from the former. What can occur is that a parade of empirical absurdities may make one more likely to entertain the thesis that the universe is also metaphysically absurd. Empirical absurdities, at best, intimate that the universe might also be metaphysically absurd.

The thesis behind metaphysical absurdity is that there is no God or sufficient reason to ground contingency in some kind of solid metaphysical necessity, but that there should have been. Even if empirical absurdities were drastically reduced, such reduction would have no bearing on whether the universe was metaphysically absurd or not. Again, such reduction in empirical absurdities could intimate that there might be an ultimate Ground, but to speak of evidence one way or the other would be inappropriate. Classical theism denies metaphysical absurdity while naturalistic humanism rejects the issue as meaningless.

To seek refuge from empirical absurdity represents a spontaneous human response, and religious belief and worship is a natural way to respond to these negative contingencies. To turn towards God, to achieve union with Brahman, to realize a state of Nirvana represent attempts to find relative stability and security in the midst of everyday life. Such religious responses arise from the empirical absurdities which descend on us.

Plato, the great seminal thinker of Western philosophy, saw our changing contingent empirical world as a "shadow" cave world of unreality from which we were to seek escape into a true world of static unchanging Forms, culminating in the Form of the Good. Plato, through the centuries, has represented the dominant strain of Western philosophical thought, and this thought, through Plotinus, was incorporated into orthodox Christian belief by Augustine in the early church. Certainty and necessity reside in God while uncertainty and contingency mark our existence in the world.

In the world of contingency and change in which we live, we are always dealing with probabilities rather than certainties. Science is fraught with probability and it runs pervasively through everyday life as well. It is true that we take many things to be certain for practical purposes, such as the rising of the sun each day, but even here we must wait on experience to see what will happen tomorrow. The great British philosopher, David Hume, showed that while we rely on regularity and repetition in life, there is no absolutely certain guarantee that regularity will continue just because it has in the past. Indeed, even with all the regularities we depend upon, the surprising and the unexpected always occur as well.

While we fortunately regard many things in everyday life as practical certainties, scientists, being more precise, always speak of the contingent world of experience in terms of various degrees of probability. For them it is not a logical certainty that the sun will rise tomorrow. For them there is an astonishingly high degree of probability that the sun will rise tomorrow, but there is still a small though negligible probability that the sun will not rise tomorrow. Fortunately, in terms of everyday life, we can ignore the negative probabilities here and in many other cases as well, but we must not lose sight of Hume's point. While he and the rest of us quite rightly rely on persistent regularities in experience, we are lucky that such regularities occur and reoccur. Even with the connections in experience which Hume denied, things just happen to occur and reoccur for us and this is fortunate. Such occurrences and recurrences do not have to occur by any laws of logic. That they happen to occur is a lucky contingency about our world. It is not logically necessary that such regularity as we find continue in the future.

Hume's unsettling insight was that logical necessity does not connect the parts of the world to each other. This lies at the heart of his analysis of causality and induction. Hume's view of the world is one of radical contingency where no real ontological connections occur at all; we make the connections. Such a world is atomistic and ultimately incoherent. There is general agreement that Hume's view of experience is too narrow and restricted. We know that there are real connections in experience, not invented by us, but the connections are not logically necessary. Gestalt psychology has demonstrated this and the views of thinkers like James and Whitehead give us a much richer and more adequate view of experience.

Peirce has also shown us that the world is lawlike, that laws are built deeply into the structure of the empirical world. Peirce's realism in regard to law is an impressive exercise in an expanded empiricism which allows us to take account of laws without seeing such laws as being logically necessary. Laws can evolve or change too, over long periods of time. Thus, the laws that apply to our world just happen to apply as do the instances that fall under them. Both in the end are contingent. Clearly there are empirical connections in our experience of the world, but the connections are not logically deductive and necessary.

Even Hume was affected by the predominating Platonic influence. His distrust of purely contingent relationships was so great that in the absence of logical necessity in experience, Hume was thrown into a radical skepticism about our knowledge of the world. This skepticism caused Hume considerable existential anguish from which he could only escape by letting nature cure him of these philosophical musings and by playing backgammon with his friends.[3] He says again and again that philosophy cannot justify the knowledge claim that there is an external world independent of our perception. It is apparent that what Hume means by "justification" is "prove with certainty." Even in Hume's time the Platonic influence that real knowledge meant certain knowledge still held sway. Philosophy could not cure this skeptical doubt for Hume, but "nature" or common sense cured him of it when he left philosophy alone. Thus, even the greatest classical empiricist was held prisoner by deeply ingrained Platonic assumptions. The discrepancy between what philosophy can show and what common sense takes for granted was an embarrassment that dogged Hume to the end of his days.

We should not be in haste to blame Hume at this point for failing to see what is now apparent to most of us. We all are victims of unconscious assumptions deeply grounded in our cultural backgrounds. One of the most difficult things to do is to uncover what Collingwood calls our "ultimate presuppositions" of thought. In our time, Hume's skepticism is seen as unwarranted because we have uncovered and largely dropped the Platonic assumption that all genuine knowledge has to be certain knowledge. Once we accept empirical knowledge and probability as legitimate cognitively, there is no basis for skepticism about the reality of the external world. Another ultimate presupposition accepted by Hume and others, but now rejected, is the Cartesian assumption that we have access only to the contents of our own minds.

Since we no longer regard contingency as a "poor relation" of necessity, Hume's skepticism about human knowledge is uncalled for. Nevertheless, Hume's genius saw something about experience which is clearly manifest and continues to cause uneasiness. The law-like nature of our world tends to hide the blunt facticity of the contingent. The world could have been different than it is, given different laws and different circumstances. Why it is as it is remains an ultimate mystery in spite of attempts to achieve a necessary Ground which would make the mystery go away.

While for practical purposes we can take for granted the high probabilities approaching certainty, it is obvious that in our dealings with the world, we are dealing with occurrences that have various degrees of antecedent probability. For practical purposes I can be certain that the sun will rise tomorrow even though there remains a small scientific probability that it will not rise. While it is also probable that my first cousin from Vancouver will arrive safely on my doorstep tomorrow, I cannot assume it as a practical certainty.

Such factors as these make people nervous and afraid of the contingent. What is contingent is also doubtful. What tomorrow will bring is questionable in various degrees and how long what is here today will remain also remains questionable and uncertain. No matter how well things are going, the "worm of doubt" always clouds the contingent with a degree of uncertainty that at best is annoying and at worst intolerable. The contingent is what happens to be the case but could have been otherwise.

We might ask, "What is so frightening about what happens to be the case?" In terms of ordinary life it is the empirical absurdities and risks in the world that cause concern. Interpreted in philosophical terms it is the *surd* character of contingent existence. The surd is what is not rationalizeable; it is what simply appears and, while part of a causal chain, is not explainable in terms of a sufficient ground or reason. No matter how extensive our causal explanation, the surd always remains unless we can achieve ultimate intelligibility which rationalists claim can be done in principle but which empiricists deny.

Contingency, since it includes the chance happening and the accidental, engenders fear and concern. In response, philosophical rationalism demanded more of the universe; it demanded ultimate intelligibility in God or Ground.

Ordinary consciousness also reacts to the insecurities of the purely contingent in terms of religious hopes for security and salvation. But ordinary consciousness does not only react to the insecurities of the purely contingent. Into the contingent world itself comes the miracle of divine impingement in various ways, drawing us on to transcend our ordinary fears and concerns.

Our dreams and hopes, indeed our very lives, do hang on tender threads which can be broken at any time. It is tempting to say that we see an ultimate rational plan to the universe which includes our good and is ultimately good and purposeful, even when bad things happen. We naturally look for an anchor in the storm of contingency. On the other hand, we can accept contingency and mystery without asking to see a plan or asking for ultimate security. This attitude can be a religious response too. Freud saw religion as only a childish desire for ultimate security in a supernatural father image. He did not entertain the possibility of a mature faith and hope in the divine, which accepts the contingent and risky as they occur. To genuinely accept a "world without why" may represent the maximum in religious trust and faith. Zen Buddhism represents the most extreme example I can think of where a religious response involving complete acceptance of the contingent is manifested. Nietzsche's response to the world may also be considered a deeply religious one, in spite of his apparent atheism. Only one who accepted contingency in all its ramifications could manifest the over-riding joy that Nietzsche felt in the idea of the eternal recurrence of the same. The suffering and the joy go together in Nietzsche. Most of us would tremble, to say the least, if faced with an endless repetition of our own lives.

While we have no choice but to face the contingencies of the world, what remains upsetting and intolerable to many is the idea that God could be contingent. It is felt that in no way could God exist by luck or chance, or just happen to exist because a certain set of circumstances occurred rather than some other set of circumstances. First of all, God is not generally felt to exist by happenstance, part of a larger environment. God is not felt to be dependent on something outside of himself in order to exist. God could not just happen to be, contingent on a certain set of circumstances, but simply must be, no matter what the circumstances.

God must be the "rock of ages" in a sea of contingent existents. God must be religiously dependable in a constant and personal sense. Nothing less than God could be so dependable. No contingent being, be it an individual, a state or a party, could be dependable in an absolute sense. To worship such contingent beings would be an act of idolatry. This is a feeling that is pervasive in religious consciousness and we shall have to see in what ways this feeling is sound and in what ways it can be very misleading.

The fear and hatred of ultimate contingency arise because outside of

God, nothing or nobody is absolutely dependable or predictable. There are degrees of dependability and predictability but in the contingent world in which we live nothing is certain. In short, contingency is fraught with risk.

Most often the search for security means turning first of all to other contingent things such as other persons, political and social organizations and the church or other religious institutions. Whether God is contingent or not is a matter of debate but the church as a human social institution seems clearly to be contingent like anything else. Money and power seem to be ways of gaining security. All such attempts at security seem motivated partly by a desperate attempt to arrest or bypass the eroding features of time.

Our own mortality and the finite duration of all our human projects are features of the contingent world that we push to the background of consciousness as much as we can. If all is contingent, there is a tendency to feel that all our projects are worthless. This widespread human dread of ultimate contingency has been a widespread phenomenon throughout history. When one stops to think about it, it seems strange that our finite projects would lose their rationale because they do not last forever. We know scientifically that, ultimately, life of any kind on earth will be impossible. We know that death will, for us, be the end of all our projects on earth, and yet such awareness does not stop us from building our own lives and, indeed, building civilizations.

Yet, throughout history, religions have given widespread expression to the human fear that exclusive devotion to finite human projects alone is pointless and depressing. There continues to be a deep human urge and longing that ultimate contingency be conquered somehow. In the West, historically at any rate, such conquest has been thought to reside in God, the ultimate non-contingent being. Perhaps such conquest consists in accepting both divinity and world in all their gift-like contingency. That is an easy thing to say, but extremely difficult to achieve.

NOTES

1. William James, "Sentiment of Rationality" in *Essays in Pragmatism* (New York: Hafner Publishing Company, 1949) p. 4.

2. Jean Paul Sartre, *Being and Nothingness* (New York: Philosophical Library, 1956) Trans. Hazel Barnes. *Nausea* (Norfolk CT: New Directions, 1950) Trans. Lloyd Alexander.

3. David Hume, *A Treatise of Human Nature* (London: Oxford University Press, 1967, Selby-Bigge edition, Part II, Section VI, Part V, Section I and II).

CHAPTER III
GIFT AND CAUSAL NECESSITY

Having given some background on the meaning of contingency, it now behooves us to discuss the characteristics of a gift. At first there does not seem to be anything startling or significant to say about them. What a gift is does not seem to be problematic or to present any issues of philosophical significance or interest. We all know what they are. On closer examination and particularly in dealing with the issue of contingency, startling and significant features begin to emerge.

The first and most important feature is that a gift is usually something we receive as freely given and not as something that appears out of duty or any other kind of necessity. It appears to us out of the blue, even if out of the goodness of someone's heart. This is not to deny that gifts are generally expected on birthdays and Christmas, that they are given repeatedly at special times of the year or that they are often expected and required among employees in various businesses. The intent of a gift is a freely given presentation from one person to another, not required out of duty or habit. Of course a gift, like anything else, does have causal antecedents and does appear at the end of a causal chain of circumstances, but it is not explicable only in these terms. To ignore the freely given aspect is to ignore its gift-carrying character. In fact, if a gift is given repeatedly only out of habit or duty, its gift-bearing character becomes considerably tarnished or vanishes.

What helps retain the gift-like character of the presentation is the element of surprise which happily can continue even in the most routine gift settings such as birthdays and Christmas. Even though we expect to receive gifts at Christmas, we hopefully do not know what we will receive specifically. Again, if the totally expected and predictable gift appears again and again, the gift-like character is tarnished. A gift should always appear with the atmosphere of magic and delight surrounding that which is not required or expected as routine.

So far we have been talking about gifts in the ordinary sense in which we speak of such things. Let us broaden the concept now to include anything which we receive as a presentation in experience that is not required or expected in the normal course of events. Ordinarily gifts can be traced back to a giver and usually we know who the giver is. We can, of course, receive anonymous gifts from an unknown giver, which makes them even more surprising and mysterious. Now let us expand this a bit further by thinking of gift characteristics that may be present even though no gift giver is assumed or known to exist.

We might wonder how this is possible since a gift generally requires a giver and a receiver. Nevertheless, it is possible to have a gift that only has a receiver, but no apparent giver.[1] A gift, to be a gift, need not necessarily have to have a clearly identifiable giver. Suppose I unexpectedly find a four leaf clover on my walk around the block. The element of surprise and pleasure may be there and it is clearly not required that I find a four leaf clover on this particular day. I may have searched in vain on other days to find such a clover. Today I find it and accept it with gratitude; it was uncalled for but a lucky find. My finding it is still a natural event like any other; it has causal antecedents and appears at the end of a causal chain. From a scientific perspective there is nothing mysterious about my finding the clover and yet an aura of surprise and joy tinges my experience at the find. Another more striking example comes to mind. Some years back my wife and

I were collecting shells on Sanibel Island in Florida; as we were walking along the beach a wave came up and suddenly deposited a perfectly formed and relatively rare tulip shell of great beauty at our feet. They are not found every day, even with hard looking, and are even less often found in perfect shape. Here, clearly, was a gift in the full sense of the term. Receivers? Yes, but no giver in the sense in which we usually think of gift givers.[2]

Many examples of gifts in this sense can be found. Experience can provide us with pleasant and unexpected surprises. Scientific research and everyday life are full of examples of lucky accidents like the discovery of radium. In these examples we have all the features of a gift except that there is no giver involved.

I would now like to widen the concept of gift somewhat in a significant way. Up to this point we have assumed that all gifts, whether from a giver or not, are value-positive and that they provide, at the least, mild pleasure or a maximum of ecstatic enjoyment depending on the nature of the gift. However, there are events and experiences which have all the features we used to characterize a gift but which, instead of being value-positive, are negative and destructive of value in their surprising impact. In terms of ordinary usage we would never call such occurrences gifts, for when speaking of gifts we intend the occurrences to be value-positive. Gifts are meant to be pleasing when there is a giver and reflect the intentions of the giver.

For our purposes it will be helpful to extend the notion of gift to include negative and destructive experiences. Having negative impact, such events have all the other features of gifts. Such gifts can range all the way from the annoying discovery one morning that we have a hemmorhoid to the sudden and tragic loss of a loved one. The element of surprise is there, the out of the blue character. Sometimes such negative experiences can turn out to be positive gifts in the long run, but this is by no means always so. Unredeemed tragedy and suffering may strike us at any time. Their gift character arises out of the suddenness and unexpectedness of the occurrences. These gifts we do not want or cherish but they are presented to us just as positive gifts are.

The trials of Job exemplify one of the most trying aspects of negative gifts which seem to have had a divine source. If God did not directly produce the trials of Job, He permitted Satan to test Job's faith by the trials presented to him. Divine punishment in this case seems unjustified because Job had done nothing to merit such punishment. In fact it seemed to be Job's godliness that led to his punishment. Satan bet God that if Job, a devout man of faith, were subjected to all kinds of trials and punishments, that he (Job) would curse God. God took Satan up on the bet and Satan lost. Aside from the questionable ethics of such a wager, were there causal reasons why God allowed all kinds of bad things to happen to Job? Presumably yes, and the primary cause was to call Satan on his bet. Whether taking the bet was ethically justifiable or not is another question.

If we grow by means of the suffering produced by negative gifts and retain our faith, as Job did, the gifts turn out to be positive. But frequently we fail the test of suffering and the burden of suffering is so intense, for many, that to speak of it as a divine negative gift seems almost blasphemous. We face another aspect of the problem of evil which seems to have no comfortable rational solution from the traditional Christian perspective.

Job's friends tried to make sense of the situation and give him comfort by trying to uncover causes for Job's sufferings that would rationalize or make sense of his experience. Surely Job was being punished for failure to be true to God. But for him, no intelligible causal reasons could make sense of the excessive misfortunes that he underwent. Here, as elsewhere, causal reasons are always operable, but are not of sufficient strength to reasonably account for the suffering undergone. What causal explanation such as backsliding could give a reasonable and morally justifiable explanation for the holocaust or the starvation and exploitation of children in the ghettos of the world? Causal reasons can be found for any phenomenon that occurs, but *justification* or intelligibility for much that occurs escapes us.

Gifts, whether positive or negative, have causal reasons, but causal reasons do not provide a justification for many gifts that we receive. The gift of divine grace is generally spoken of as unmerited in the sense of not being an obvious effect of precedent causes. Negative gifts, such as those Job received, were clearly unmerited too in terms of Job's previous life. Any gift presumably has causes and in the case of divine gifts, these causes must still be separated from the justification for the gifts.

Causal reasons for gifts are different from justifications for giving gifts. When speaking of divine grace, orthodox Christians consider that there is no justification for such grace. Since in their view grace is unmerited, there is no justification for its dispensation. Because of sin, we don't deserve grace, but God may choose to dispense it anyway. This does not mean that God does something bad when He bestows grace. When one says that there is no justification for grace we mean there are no rational reasons, including deserving it, for grace being given. Divine grace is probably the most profound gift that Christians can receive gratis.

Are there causal reasons why divine grace is bestowed? Probably, but most of them are unknowable by us. It is possible and even likely that petitionary prayer and good works sometimes operate as causal reasons. Whether they ever are causally efficacious is a matter of considerable dispute among Christians. If such causal reasons are present to divinity they certainly don't necessitate the gift of grace or there would be no gift at all.

There are causal reasons for gifts as there are causal reasons for anything else. Yet if one could give a full set of causal reasons for a gift being given, the gift is still not necessitated by those causal reasons. If it were necessitated it would no longer be a gift. A gift is something more than a simple or complex effect that results from a simple or complex causal chain. As we shall see shortly, a gift is an emergent, something new and special which has appeared, not required by the causal chain itself.

When talking about divine gifts, good or bad, we remain profoundly ignorant of the causal conditions involved. Orthodox Christians would say that this is because there are no causal conditions with divine gifts. God is completely outside the causal order. This is why God is spoken of as supernatural. Yet, if divinity manifests itself in the empirical world then divine actions and gifts ought to fall within the causal order. It is a major contention of this study that divinity is manifested in the empirical world, though in very special ways, to be sure. Reductionistic empiricism would say that divine manifestation does fall within the causal order but it would hold that all such reports of divine manifestation are explicable as delusions or hallucinations of some kind. Physiological, psychological and sociological explanations of divine gifts of grace can be given and we can try to explain them in purely causal terms.

However, there are various reasons for rejecting a reductionistic empiricism of this kind as profoundly inadequate in accounting for divine manifestation. First of all, such a reductionism is not coherent with the mass of phenomenological data concerning religious experience.[3] Such reductionism falsifies and distorts the phenomenological picture. The data on this is massive. Many so-called religious experiences no doubt are delusive and can often be shown to be so, but to brand all accounts of religious experience as delusive flies in the face of too much data which has been amassed since humans were on earth.

To regard divinity as supernatural, outside the world of experience altogether, is to desert any attempt to bring an empirical methodology to bear on these questions. Even if divinity ingresses into the world from some supernatural domain, once manifested, divine impingement calls for some kind of philosophical explication.

While divine impingement is very special and unusual, the gift of grace must have some similarities to other gifts or there would be no way to talk about it at all. Since divinity is a hidden consciousness, most of what constitutes divine action will remain unknown and unknowable by us. If God has reasons for dispensing gifts, these reasons remain hidden from us.

Recognizing the limitations involved here, it is not too far-fetched to say that both prayer and good works could sometimes be causal factors in divine grace and the way it operates. If they could not be causal factors at all, they would be meaningless as religious practices. However, if the connection were *only* causal, religious practices would degenerate into magic. Magic involves what are thought to be simple causal chains which turn out to be erroneous on further examination. In either case magic involves causal chains and nothing else. "Do y, and x results." "Utter the secret password or rub the bottle and the genie will appear."

Prayer and good works on the other hand are not magic practices. They attempt to persuade another consciousness to do something. Persuasion is a causal reason, but it is more than that as well. If you hope to persuade divinity to do something by praying for it or performing good works, the divine gift does not automatically follow because the persuasion may not work. A simple cause produces its effects. Persuasion, on the other hand, while causal, does not always produce the desired effects. The persuasion may not work. Both prayer and good works present some kind of justification which the worshipper hopes will causally have some influence on divinity.

If we are to regard religion as empirically based at all, it would seem that we should regard divine manifestations as natural rather than supernatural occurrences. We should regard such manifestations as occurring inside the causal order. I am aware that this idea runs counter to what many religious thinkers believe. Such a supposition seems to reduce divinity to just another contingent item of experience, and yet it is hard to make sense out of prayer and meditation unless divinity operates within the causal order. Later in this study we shall see reason to hold that, even though contingent, divinity is not just another contingent item of the universe. It is also evident that how divinity operates and why is largely unknown.

However, if prayer and meditation have any meaning at all, it would seem essential to hold that in some way or other, divinity can receive causal influences from the world. Whitehead, among others, has thought so and he called this aspect of divinity God's consequent nature. That divinity can receive causal influences from the world does not mean that such influences necessitate divine actions in specific ways any more than causal influence necessitates particular human actions. To borrow a phrase from an earlier time in philosophy, "Causes can incline but not necessitate."

Buber talks about the human to human encounter as an I-Thou encounter and he describes the divine-human encounter in the same terms. In encounter, whether between human and human or between God and humans, mutual causal influence takes place, but it takes place between free beings. If x influences y then y also influences x. Though the influence may be mutual, the relation is not symmetrical, particularly if one of the terms is God. While we indeed can influence God in the I-Thou encounter, His influence on us is vast and multifaceted, and of a very special nature indeed. He influences us in ways we could never influence Him.

Returning to the issue of causality in general, causes refer to antecedent conditions that helped bring something about, but in the case of intentional actions do not give a full account of the action as gift. If junior gives his sister a toy only because he has been told to by his parents, the causal explanation is complete but the gift-bearing character is gone as far as junior is concerned, though it may still be seen as a gift by his sister. If we talk only of antecedent causes of an action, we speak of the action as routine or mechanical. If the action involves a gift from a giver, then we must speak of the giver's intention as well as of the receiver's possible reaction.

One aspect of gifts is particularly evident in gambling games like poker. Here we speak of it as "lady luck." Sometimes we win and sometimes we lose. In games of luck and chance, as in the rest of life, luck does not entail a lack of causal determinism. There is a complicated set of causal conditions which make the dice fall as they do; their chance character resides in the fact that we cannot know all the causal conditions, thus, the gift-like character and surprise when we see how the dice fall. Also, the fall of honest dice does not involve any intentional factor as cause, while loaded dice, on the other hand, are those where an intentional factor has been introduced, unknown to one of the players.

For our purposes we need not try to decide the issue of hard determinism or soft determinism. In either case, the gift-like character of the throw of the dice is apparent or there would be no game to play. Gifts, whether positive or negative, continue to manifest the characteristics we have talked about so far. Games of chance are particularly good examples to bring out both the value-positive and value-negative aspects of gifts. What applies to games of chance applies also to life as a whole, except that in life more intentional factors and multiple causes come into play. We no longer have pure chance, but an element of luck or chance still remains. In life the surprising, the unexpected and the new turn up continuously.

In summing up our discussion of gifts so far, we can say that a gift, though part of a perfectly natural causal chain, breaks in on us unexpectedly and does not seem strictly required or predictable in terms of what has taken place up to that point. We will apply this concept to contingency as such later on, but for now we must look at some further characteristics of gifts.

We may get some more insight into the nature of gifts by looking briefly at the concept of action. To act is to deliberately carry out an intention on the part of a human being or higher animal organism such as a dog or a cat. Acts are attributed primarily to human beings but animals can act too. I act when I deliberately mail a letter at the post office and a dog can act when it bites the postman who delivers the letter. If, on the other hand, a tile falls off the roof and knocks the postman out, no direct act is involved. The tile didn't do anything.

The significant thing about actions is that they are deliberate; they involve an intention on the part of the one who acts. Many actions are gifts too, but most are not seen to be so. If I put bolt x in hole y on an assembly line, it is an action, but it is not seen as a gift. Most importantly, if one undertakes an action, whether it be to fill a coffee cup or to raise the debt ceiling, one has initiated a *new* series of events that would not have occurred if the action had not been taken. By acting I introduce something new into the world, a new causal series which will continue to produce effects into the future. In a special and peculiar sense, an act, by its very nature, can be seen as a special kind of gift. This is because, by acting, I initiate a new series of causal events that would not have occurred if I had not acted. Thus, there is a potential gift-like character to deliberate action, provided there is a potential receiver.[4]

In any action there is what I can only call an emergent factor. By this I mean that an action introduces something new into the causal situation that was not present before. Of course, a purely mechanical type of behavior can introduce something new that wasn't there before also, but in mechanical behavior the new factor is something that is just the end result of the causal process and is completely explicable in purely causal terms. If I push bolt x into hole y, I produce something new that wasn't there before; it is an action, but my behavior is completely explicable by what has gone before in terms of the training and orders I have been given by my superiors and by other aspects of the job situation I am in. A robot can do as well.

If I take some initiative and reorganize the performance of a job in a way I have thought out for myself, the new action is a genuine emergent. To make sense of it I still have to look at previous causes as I do in the first case. But now, nothing leading up to my action will completely explain my reorganizing the job the way I did. My action could have gone in a number of directions before I acted. But by my reorganization something really new emerges in the situation. This emergent aspect is not some mysterious non-empirical property that inheres in significant actions as opposed to routine actions. The emergent aspect is something we all recognize in significant actions when we say that in the end, "He did it" or "He didn't do it." It is significant actions that are regarded as peculiarly mine and which can be attributed to me as a person, unique from anyone else.

It is important to note, however, that though I initiate a new series of events by acting, it is still the case that my act is also the result of a previous causal series at the same time. I or someone else may not know the reason why I acted as I did but, if necessary, psychologists and other social scientists can look into my action and come up with reasons leading up to it. The paradoxical though apparently true situation seems to be that my action is both the end result of a previous causal series and, at the same time, the beginning of a new causal series. A deliberate action always has prior factors which led up to it, just as does any other event, but the action itself is mine. It initiates something new and, thus, has the potential character of a gift. When I act, my act cannot only be explained as the result of a previous causal series, but I can also be held morally and legally accountable for the action as being mine.

In a sense my act is both determined and free at the same time, an apparent contradiction, but, nevertheless, the case. This issue is one of the most perplexing in moral philosophy, affecting both ethics and law. There is no clear and easy solution to this paradox, but for our purposes it is apparent that actions must be described in this way in order to make any sense out of them. In law, if I successfully plead insanity as a defense, my lawyer is saying that what I did was no longer an action, but only an end result of a causal series. If I cannot plead insanity, then the act is attributed to me and I am held responsible for it, even though the determining factors from the past are still operative. There are two ways of looking at an action. In one sense it can be free and in another it is determined.

We can meaningfully say two things at the same time: "I know the reasons why you did that (and they causally determine your action), but you still should not have done it. (You are in some sense free of these causal influences)." We are faced with an apparent contradiction. If there is really something I should or should not do, this can only make sense if I can either do it or refrain from doing it. No matter which free choice I make, there is also a set of causal determining reasons which can be given for the choice. There are ways of dealing with this paradox, but to pursue the matter further here would take us outside the bounds of this study.

Think about the difference between kicking somebody intentionally and kicking a person by accident. Both are natural events in that both can be described as the end result of a previous causal series, though the series will be different in the two cases. Both causal series lead to the event called "kicking someone." The behavior may be identical in the two cases, but in the one case I kicked deliberately and in the other case by accident. In both cases the question can be asked, "Why did the kick occur?" In both cases an answer can be given in terms of antecedent casual conditions. But in the case of a deliberate kick, the same question can be asked but a different answer is expected. Knowing the factors that led up to the kick, we can still ask, "Why the hell did you kick me?" If the kick was deliberate we have some more explaining to do. If it was an accident we usually say, "Oh, I am sorry" thereby indicating that though a kick has indeed occurred and was somehow caused, it was not an action in the sense of something carried out with deliberate intent.

Where is all this discussion leading? The point is that deliberate action brings out, in a striking way, some significant features of a gift. A deliberate action introduces an element of intent or purpose; a gift must either have a giver who intends the gift or a receiver who accepts the gift whether there is a giver or not. Once an action is carried out, we may be faced with a new gift presentation with which we will have to deal.

Actions and gifts have certain significant features. Both are emergent and bring something new to a situation that is not solely a result of causal influences from the past. Both have causal antecedents though such antecedents may remain unknown. Causes have influences on actions and gifts but they do not necessitate either the action or the gift. Even in the most routine action such as putting bolt x in hole y and where it seems that the action is just a result of preceding conditioning, one day I may wake up and decide not to put bolt x in hole y.

However, as we shall see, there is one gift which is not an action, that can have no discernable causal antecedents. This is the gift of contingency itself — that anything whatsoever exists.

NOTES

1. You can have gifts with givers but no receivers too, gifts that are offered but not accepted.

2. You might speak of finding something after long effort and not think of it in gift-like terms at all. How about finding King Tut's tomb? Is this a gift? Perhaps not in the usual sense and yet there is the surprise of finding it. Logic and experience do not require that if you seek you will find. Success is still in some sense a gift, and it is this aspect that is of concern in our study. The Gospels promise, "Seek and ye shall find" but the finding is truly a gift, not logically required by searching.

3. See my *Intimations of Divinity*, Chapters 4 and 5.

4. While metaphysically all deliberate actions introduce a new emergent series into the world producing a potential gift quality, psychologically many actions can still be repetitive and unsurprising, thus, not appearing as gift-like. In a sense, all actions might be considered gifts metaphysically, but in the empirical day to day world, most actions are not considered gifts.

CHAPTER IV
EXPERIENCE AS A GIFT

It is clear from what we have said that only portions of our experience could be considered gifts. Most of the time, experience is routine, repetitive and quite ordinary. It is interspersed with surprises of varying degrees of intensity but most of the time experience is simply taken for granted. The routines of ordinary life have a predictable character that allow us to function with a reasonable degree of efficiency.

In the middle of a battle, experience is fraught with constant surprises of a negative character, and if relief does not come soon enough, battle fatigue closes in. Christmas morning is generally one of constant surprises as the pleasant gift aspect of experience becomes obviously dominant. Yet, how would one feel if the influx of gifts on Christmas morning continued unabated for a month? As children, this would seem like heaven, but as thoughtful adults we realize that such an experience would lose its intense value-positive quality, leading at best to ordinary boredom and, at worse, to driving you "out of your gourd." Constant surprise would soon become intolerable.

If everything were a gift, even in the extended senses we developed, nothing would seem to be a gift, for there would be no contrast with the non-gift, and the term would lose its applicability. A gift can only stand out or be noticed against the background of the usual and expected, which is not a gift. Thus, given the things and events that appear in our experience on earth, while they are all contingent, only some would appear to be gifts. Thus, in the way we ordinarily speak, most things are not seen as gifts. We have departed from ordinary usage, extending the term "gift" much more widely than is usual. We must examine how the term could be applied to everything without becoming empty of meaning and vacuous.

So far we have given a straightforward explication of what it is to be contingent and what it is to be a gift. I would now like to take us into deeper philosophical waters by exploring possible usages of the term "gift" that depart quite radically from usages we have been concerned with up to this point. Suppose we consider for a moment the planet earth which we generally take for granted. Recall how the earth looked to the first astronauts who saw it from outer space. Recall how it looked to us on our television screens in living color. From the descriptions given by our men in space, it would appear that the sight was awe-inspiring indeed, and it would not seem far out of line to say that, at that moment, they experienced the earth as a gift, uncalled for, surprising and overwhelming. Many of us who saw the scene on television experienced it as a gift too, though obviously to a lesser degree of intensity than did the men in space.

Let us take a more familiar example. We experience the moon in various ways and in various contexts, many of them quite ordinary and not noteworthy. But how about when we experience it at special times as a harvest moon or in romantic contexts? It would not be far-fetched to say that on such occasions the moon could appear to us as a gift.

What both examples illustrate is that the gift-like character of something may also depend on how it is taken by the receiver. A giver could intend that something be a gift, but the receiver might not see it as one. In most gift-like situations such as Christmas, there is not much leeway for interpretation on the part of the receiver or giver. In situations where gifts are not expected to be given or received, there is more latitude for various interpretations.

If you have been extremely ill for some time, when you begin to recover the first meal you can hold down appears very strongly as a gift, though ordinarily meals do not, particularly hospital meals. Of more significance is the fact that after a protracted, severe illness from which one has barely recovered, the entire range of experience may appear as a gift. We gratefully accept the experience of being alive as something uncalled for and unexpected. This mood does not usually last very long as we sink back into the routine of the ordinary, but such experiences do occur and they are philosophically very significant.

The feeling that our entire range of experience is a gift is a radical departure from our usual attitudes and, as we saw, tends to deprive the term "gift" of clear meaning, since there is nothing with which to contrast it. Nevertheless, examination of the thesis that all experience is a gift is important because of the philosophical and religious implications involved.

Could we sustain the feeling continuously that experience, taken as a whole, is a gift? We have already seen that most things are not gifts, that is, every particular thing in the world, taken one at a time, is not a gift. But now the question is asked in a collective sense. Can the totality of experience be considered a gift? Most people, I suspect, would say "no."

For most persons, whether they are religious or not, the issue is not raised. Most of us, most of the time, do not think of experience as a gift. In extreme situations like those we mentioned earlier such as recovering from a severe illness, experience may temporarily seem a gift but the mood soon passes. In the temporary period, however, the gift-like features manifest themselves strongly whether one is religious or not.

There are a number of persons, however, who would answer our question by saying "yes." These people would regard the totality of experience as being literally the gift of God or else they would see experience as a gift without a giver.

The gift-like character of experience may be an implicit feature of theistic faith and possibly of religious awareness as such. After all, for orthodox Christians, God did create the world out of nothing and there was no necessity that he do so. Experience, for orthodox Christians, should presumably always be seen as a gift from God. While *theologically* experience may be so considered, it is not felt *experientially* to be so by most of us. It is hard to see how we could see all experience this way unless we were in a relatively rare spiritual state of mind. For those who are religious, whether expressed in orthodox terms or not, it would seem that, at least implicitly, experience should be considered a gift. This may seem a persuasive idea when applied to value-positive experiences but is open to considerable doubt in the case of negative experiences such as pain, suffering and tragedy. These experiences are generally thought of as anything but gift-like. The only gift involved would be God's grace which would appear to mitigate or remove the negative experiences. Possibly the suffering might be seen as a gift because you could learn from it.

It is sometimes said that suffering is an opportunity for growth or development; indeed, it is sometimes said that we can grow only through suffering. While this saying is often repeated endlessly as an old bromide in a simplistic and patronizing way, there may be more to it than meets the eye. Saints and mystics are not like most of us; their spiritual sensitivity is honed much more finely than ours. What many of them suggest is that all experience, value-negative as well as value-positive, be seen as a gift from divinity. I use the term, "divinity," here rather than "God" because I am referring to non-theistic as well as theistic religions.[1]

There is an old Chinese proverb put in the form of a question. It says, "How can I escape the fire?" The answer given is, "Go into the very center of the flame." This proverb seems paradoxical and perverse to say the least. Yet, what seems to be intended here is the idea that our own worst fears and negative experiences may be a condition of our growth and salvation, the negative side of the divine gift. The Chinese have propounded the doctrine of the yin and the yang for centuries. Yin and yang represent the opposites, good and bad. Both require each other and both are part of the divine gift of experience.

Hindu and Buddhist theology seem much more willing than the Christian West to accept the negative and the positive as divine gifts. While many Christian saints and mystics seem just as sensitive to this point as their counterparts in the East, much Christian theology tends to set up a radical dualism between good and evil, personified by God and Satan respectively. The added message is that we should side with God and reject Satan. If the saints and mystics are right, however, as against the theologians, then it is Satan, too, in the form of the negative, that is the source of our salvation. This is a difficult thing to understand, let alone accept.

Let us take a simple case. Suppose I grew up with an inordinate fear of dogs, a fear strong enough to almost incapacitate me for functioning in the world. This is in a sense, my "devil." If I can deal with this fear in a creative way I can presumably overcome it. I overcome it not by rejecting my fear and simply trying to suppress it, but by accepting it as actual and in some manner trying to come to terms with it. If I can incorporate my "devil" into my life in some fashion, I will not only overcome this fear but it will make me better able to come to terms with other "devils" that I have.

It would seem as though we should "go into the center of the flame" and accept it too as a gift of divinity. Much modern psychology seems to bear this out, arguing that the way to mental health is to come to terms with our negative and dark sides, our own devils.

Accepting the negative as gift still sounds paradoxical, however. The view that everything is a divine gift still has a stumbling block of major proportions. How do we deal with the holocaust? It is one thing to accept and deal with my own shortcomings but something else to accept the holocaust and other moral outrages as a divine gift. Can one seriously regard moral outrages, too, as a gift? The enormity of the holocaust staggers the imagination and defies any attempt to make it rationally and morally comprehensible. When we add to this the nearly equal butcheries of Stalin and other moral absurdities of our time, to call such events gifts seems blasphemy to say the least.

In spite of what saints and mystics might say, we find it difficult to accept the idea that such events are part of the divine gift of experience. It seems too easy and morally unacceptable to respond that the "gift" of the holocaust is simply a mystery that surpasses human understanding but that it all works out in the sight of God. What scheme of things, including the will of God, could justify the torture and death endured by so many?

I can only speculate that the ability to regard experience as a gift is itself a gift. To be able to call experience a gift at all may only occur by the grace of God or divinity on a one on one basis. For us to hold the belief that all experience is a gift, as a general statement, true for all persons, is absurd. Between a person and God, divinity's gift-character may be private.

We cannot ask whether experience is a gift in a general and public sense. Our response is usually pragmatic. To view experience as a gift is to move beyond the purely utilitarian response to it. To be able to see experience as a gift is to regard life as ultimately valuable and to embrace it in both its good and bad aspects. While this would seem to be a response appropriate to theists, it is a response that can be made by atheists as well. Nietzsche accepted all of life, the good and the bad, with open enthusiasm; his was a life with a great amount of suffering and pain, ending in madness, and devoid of God. There is no question that he regarded all experience as a gift, though without a giver, but perhaps, unknown to Nietzsche, the gift of seeing experience this way was bestowed on him.

We might go on to ask why we should accept as a gift the stupidities and immoral behavior that man produces. Why not accept as gift only value-positive experiences? Unfortunately, positive and negative experiences cannot be separated from each other this neatly;[2] the causal connections between experiences are too interwoven. We can only say that if experience, including the holocaust, is a gift, God and man undergo it together, and a limited God, though not implicated in evil, must suffer the effects of evil as a consequence of man's learning experiences.

Viewing the relation of God to man as analogous to that of parent and child may prove helpful. Parent and child are finite, and a loving parent can only do so much to persuade a child. What the child does, then, is undergone or suffered by both parent and child. The more the parent loves the child, the more suffering the parent undergoes as the child works through his or her problems.

Though the distance between man and divinity is vastly greater than that between a parent and a child, both may be forced to confront the consequences of choices made by man, be they good or bad. The gift of experience, as undergone by both man and God, may bring both into close community. Many times suffering binds people together in community; perhaps the same applies to the community of man and God. There is still no easy answer to the holocaust question. The price paid still seems too terrible to make any sense or to be justified. What is astonishing to note, however, is that some in the death camps felt strongly supported in the loving arms of God in the midst of the most terrible of experiences. This was probably not true of most, but that it occurred at all is astonishing.

Let us go back to a point we took up earlier. If experience as a whole is a gift, doesn't this remove the element of surprise we find with particular gifts? How can anything be considered a gift if the element of surprise is absent? For those who do think experience as a whole is a gift, an element of surprise *is* constantly present. Such persons are continuously grateful and surprised that experience as such appears to be given to them. Their gratitude to God or the universe that any world occurs at all, continues to be manifested in prayer, meditation and thanksgiving. In addition to being a divine dispensation, it requires a peculiar and unusual intensity of religious awareness to view experience as a whole this way. Thus, it could be argued that Nietzsche was a profoundly religious thinker even though he thought of himself as an atheist. This point is worthy of development, though this is not the place to do it.[3]

Whether experience is regarded as a gift or not, it is clearly both value-positive and value-negative. We respond to it with various feelings of joy, dread, hope, fear and faith in the future. For many, the mixed character of experience is accepted as routine and to be dealt with in the appropriate way on a piecemeal basis.

It is worthy of note that certain types of religious consciousness recoil in horror from ordinary experience, regarding it as sinful and wicked and anything but gift-like. Such persons feel we should flee from the wicked world into the arms of God. In this type of religious awareness, experience is not seen as a gift at all. Early Buddhism recoiled from experience as a vale of tears, where suffering was regarded as the main feature of life. In such a situation one sought to escape the world through meditation and enter into a state of mystical fulfillment.

If experience can be seen as a religious gift, why is it that experience is rejected as non gift-like by many mystics and religious thinkers? Perhaps they fear contingency as much or more than the rest of us. The contingent world is regarded by many as the prime source of temptation from the religious path of enlightenment.

Some of this rejection in Western religion can be traced back to the strong Platonic influence in Christianity. For Plato, the static Forms set standards of precision and perfection which the contingent world could never match. Eternal values set unchanging standards against which we measure the contingent, changing, moral choices of everyday life. For many, an eternal unchanging Formlike reality constituted the ontological status of God. Such a being could be the only real source of security.

If all experience can be seen as a gift from God by some, why is it that everyday experience is often seen as a threat to spiritual growth or a source of sin and wickedness? Divine impingement does not generally force us into states of consciousness that we resist. For most of us, experience is fraught with danger and risk, with trials which we must overcome. We are unable to receive this particular gift from God, and must receive divine disclosure in other ways. Perhaps this is why the world as experienced is often contrasted with a lost paradise, a garden of Eden or a golden age where men were pure and sinless.

The loss of a golden age of innocence is one of the great myths of mankind and appears in various forms outside the Judeo-Christian tradition as well as within it. Empirically, the myth is a response to the fact that humans are eternally discontented with their conditions of existence in the contingent world. We have a continuing urge to flee it or to transcend it. Empirically, one of the most significant aspects of the human condition is that we find the world dissatisfying in varying degrees, and the more developed we become the more dissatisfaction manifests itself. The urge to transcend our human condition is strong. This urge made Plato and others postulate that we were once in an ideal state from which we have fallen into the risky state of our worldly contingency. A frequent response has been to attempt to flee from this contingent world into a secure static world of changeless eternal truths. The urge to transcendence must be recognized and respected, but to flee from contingency is only one of a number of responses that can be made to this urge.[4] It should be recognized that the drive to flee headlong from contingency was usually viewed as heretical. From the viewpoint of this study, to flee the empirical world is an erroneous response.

Erroneous or not, a sizable number of Christian mystics have turned against the world, seeing it as the place where we have sinned and which we must put behind us. This negative attitude towards the contingent world is also found very strongly manifested in Hinduism and Buddhism.

The sound intuition at the core of the negativism is the realization on the part of these saints and mystics that we are called to be radically better than we are. To put it this way may sound odd but basically the idea is that something within us urges us or pulls on us to transcend ourselves and perfect ourselves to a degree that far surpasses our ability just to survive in this world. This urge may be relatively weak in most of us, but is a marked driving force in the lives of saints and mystics. Rightly or wrongly they feel that to transcend this world, one must reject it. The conclusion that they draw is understandable but highly questionable. In the negative tradition that flees the world, one interprets the message of transcendence as saying that the contingent world of experience is bad. As we shall see later, this is not the only message or, indeed, necessarily the correct message to be drawn.

For some mystics, rejection of the world is purely negative, reflecting fear of the contingent and the changing. However, there can be a positive aspect to world rejection, namely, the urge to transcend the world, expressed in the desire to exceed and develop in spiritual fulfillment beyond what can be reasonably expected of anyone given our empirical conditions of existence in the world. This state is not to be confused with arrogant egoistic pride.

This positive approach would accept and develop the urge for transcendence without finding it necessary to reject the contingent world in the process. Material goods would be accepted and enjoyed for all that they can bring, but at the same time, the goods of the world would point towards values and aspirations that cannot be realized by simple reliance on material things. From the fact that we may be called on to be better than we are, it does not follow that we must totally reject the way we are or the goods that ordinary experience can realize. The message need not be to reject experience and contingency, but to accept them for what they are and to push through them to something more fulfilling than what ordinary life has to offer. In the positive approach, one may end up by having the best of both worlds — contingent experience and transcendence.

Rejecting or accepting the world for the purpose of transcending it does not exhaust the religious options. The third religious attitude we have looked at in this chapter (taking all experience as a gift) accepts the world in all its givenness as indeed gift-like. Zen Buddhism, for example, openly accepts experience in an attitude which seems markedly different from that of the Buddha himself. Those in the Zen tradition embrace experience with an open acceptance that is unusual and quite different from the way the Buddha recoiled from it. Zen meditation practices attempt to shortcut theorizing and seek to heighten the simple gift-like awareness of all experience. In some ways, Zen is the most radical attempt that has been made to enter fully into experience, taking all experience as a gift rather than fleeing from it. Zen also appears to make the attempt to induce this state by rigorous meditation practices rather than receive it as a gift of divinity on a one on one basis.

We have argued that the ability to see all of experience as a gift is itself a gift, given by God. Yet, if Zen Buddhists are correct, it looks as though we ought to be able to induce the ability to see all experience as a gift on our own by rigorous meditation practices. The two approaches are not as diametrically opposed as might appear at first. My understanding of Zen is that though very rigorous and bizarre meditation practices are undertaken, they are not intended to take heaven by storm. The attempt is to "bracket" or set aside the natural and pragmatic attitude where logical and intellectual thought processes predominate. Once this barrier is removed, it is thought that we would be open to seeing experience as a gift. The logical puzzles or *koans* that the Zen masters give to their disciples are designed to "break" the rational intellect, so that the feeling component of our experience can fully enter our consciousness.

Zen masters contend that it is our ordinary rational and pragmatic thought processes that hinder us from receiving the full brunt of experience as gift. Pragmatic thought filters out most of what we experience in order for us to get on with the required practices of everyday life. The filters can also be removed by taking hallucinogenic drugs, but this is a risky procedure often having no relation to the spiritual life. Unless seen in a religious context of spiritual growth, removing the filters by drugs only gives you a "high" and "blows your mind" temporarily, often followed by negative "downers."

Zen meditation is fully aware of the dangers of removing the filters of experience outside the context of rigorous attempts at spiritual growth. In the context of the worshipful community, opening oneself to the full range of experience can lead to the gift of seeing all experience as a gift. Even the use of drugs can be helpful if used in the context of community group worship. Many cultures have incorporated both the careful use of drugs and meditation practices in order to facilitate seeing all experience as a gift.[5]

In any case, when rigorous meditation practices are undertaken, the most that can be accomplished is to remove the filters that ordinary consciousness puts up. Then either experience will be seen as a gift or it will not. The gift character must still emerge from the experience itself. Removal of the filters cannot produce the feeling of experience as a gift, as a cause produces its effect. For the Zen Buddhist, the world that is experienced now is not different from one seen before, but is the same world seen in a new light. Zen Buddhists illustrate the world being seen in a new light with their series of ten cow-herding pictures, a device for illustrating spiritual growth. In the first picture we see a boy riding a water buffalo. In the pictures that follow, we see a series of changes culminating in a blank sheet for picture nine. This is not the end of the series. In picture ten, we again see the boy riding the water buffalo. It is the same world we saw in picture one and yet it is not, for now it is seen in a new light.

Translating these Zen insights into Western terms, we could say that meditation practices may help put us in a frame of mind where we are more open than before to divine disclosure. These practices can not *make* us see all experience as a gift; the disclosure must still come from God. Furthermore, it would seem that meditation practices or drug taking are not necessary conditions for seeing experience this way. God can and does bestow this gift on some who have never engaged in such practices. It is a rare gift, bestowed on only a few, but a treasured one.

We might ask, "Why does the ability to see experience in a special way necessarily come from God?" Perhaps a few people are more in tune with their surroundings than the rest of us. We certainly could not prove that the ability to view all experience as a gift must come from God. Nevertheless, it is interesting to note that most people who report seeing experience as a gift regard themselves as being the recipients of a rare favor for which they are most grateful. They feel as though some kind of giver is involved and rarely, if ever, regard their view of experience as being brought about solely by their own efforts.

There are some in the Zen tradition and elsewhere who fall into the trap of thinking that various practices of worship can causally induce such disclosure, but the profoundest spiritual leaders and Zen masters feel that this is not so. To regard all experience as a gift due to our own efforts alone tends to produce spiritual pride leading to the loss of the ability to see experience as a gift. In the end we can only be open to what may occur.

The more moderate and usual positive way of viewing experience we spoke of earlier accepts the demands of both contingency and transcendence; we do not turn against the contingent world nor do we accept it all as a gift. We seek to transcend the world while also accepting the world with all its contingencies. The third way (taking all experience to be a gift) is much more radical and, in being an extreme view, has something in common with the purely negative way which rejects the world completely. Like those who reject the world completely, those who accept all of the world as a gift have relatively few practitioners, but those few have something important to tell us.

One apparent problem with such radical acceptance is that it seems to make no moral distinction between good and bad, but accepts all experience as being a gift. People in this frame of mind are generally loath to make ethical judgments of comparative value, ruling out some experiences as morally unacceptable. Nevertheless, they should make a distinction between accepting an experience and endorsing it. There is a sense in which a kind and loving parent fully accepts and receives the child's tantrums without endorsing them. Indeed, such a parent can act to reduce the chances of tantrums in the future. In a similar way saints and mystics may accept the world in all its mixed horrors and blessings without necessarily endorsing all that occurs. Such acceptance was manifested by Jesus on the cross when he said, "Forgive them for they know not what they do."

Strict moralists in their concern to judge immoral behavior and action often comdemn and reject the perpetrators as well as the actions. The trick of spiritual growth is to be able to accept the perpetrator of the crime as a child of God while rejecting the crime. This is something that most of us cannot do and most of us would find morally impossible to do in respect to the mass murderers of mankind such as Hitler and Stalin. But to those who are given the gift of seeing all of experience as gift, acceptance of the world without necessary endorsement seems possible. It is important, however, that those who accept the third view do not lose their sense for moral distinctions in the process. How to maintain the ability to morally condemn what should be condemned without rejecting the persons who perform the actions remains one of the most difficult and puzzling requirements of the spiritual life.

There is an ambivalence and oddity about the religious response to the world. On the one hand there emerges a tendency to accept experience with trust and confidence as being a gift of God while more usual is a tendency to either fear and distrust the world of experience as a vale of tears from which we must flee, or else we seek to transcend the world by pursuing goals of self-fulfillment that the world is not geared to satisfy. Many, who do not see all experience as gift, search for the non-contingent and the certain in a God who is regarded as necessarily existent, lacking the features of contingency. God is seen as a rock on which we can rely, a rock grounded in necessity, rescuing us from the changing and uncertain world of contingent experience. The more non gift-like the world appears, the more there is a tendency for all of us to throw ourselves on a divinity that is believed to be certain and necessary.

NOTES

1. Non-theistic religions teach that the universe is governed by a spiritual force or forces of a positive nature which we can tap into by various methods of meditation and self-discipline. These forces are often conceived of quite vaguely but what separates them from theistic religions is that the latter embrace a supreme personalistic being called God. One can find various kinds of non-theistic religions in Hinduism and Buddhism as well as in certain kinds of nature mysticism.

2. We are faced with what is called the paradox of hedonism. One would like to accept good experiences and reject bad ones but one finds that either one must be open to all experience and suffer or else withdraw from all experience like the Stoics and feel nothing.

3. Only a religious type of consciousness could cry out, as Nietzsche did, that "God is dead and we have killed him." The truly non-religious person is uninterested in religious questions. Nietzsche was deeply concerned with the God question. Even though he was an atheist, the question of God was a burning one for him, a truly live option in James's sense of the term. In his doctrine of eternal recurrence, he urges us to accept all of the contingent events of our lives as gifts, but without a giver. Such acceptance, however, tends to put Nietzsche's position "beyond good and evil," which creates a real problem about ethics.

4. See Chapter IX.

5. C. J. Ducasse, *A Philosophical Scrutiny of Religion* (New York: Ronald Press, 1953) p. 306; Aldous Huxley, *The Doors of Perception* (New York: Harper Colophon Books, 1963).

CHAPTER V
THE FELT DEFICIENCIES OF A CONTINGENT GOD

Most religious thinkers find ultimate contingency unacceptable for reasons which we looked at earlier.[1] There is general acceptance that the world of experience is contingent, but it is generally felt that the contingency of the world must be grounded in a being that is not contingent, namely God. If experience is contingent and God manifests Himself in human experience, it would seem that God would be contingent too. Why, then, has it been widely felt that God must exist necessarily?

Religiously, God is regarded as the supreme Being, lord over all that exists. Such supremacy seems threatened if God is accepted as contingent. A contingent being is one that could conceivably fail to exist, indeed one that will probably cease to exist at some time or other. That such a situation should apply to God, the Lord of heaven and earth, is generally regarded as intolerable. It has been widely felt that only God's necessary unsurpassability and supremacy can serve as a guarantee against such an eventuality. There are, however, theologians who do not speak of divine supremacy in this way. A number prefer to speak of God's perfections in other terms, rejecting the notion of abstract logical necessity. Barth, for example, says:

> We have to ask ourselves whether the confidence with which we think we can speak of the necessity of the

> existence of God can resist the challenge of the question which inevitably arises, whether God might also not be, or be other than He is? The genuine necessity to answer this question negatively can spring only from the God who knows no necessity, who, not needing His being, simply has being as a matter of empirical fact, thus affirming Himself in fact, although He does not need to, as the One who is.[2]

If there were one contingent God, why not a plurality of contingent gods? Why one supreme being? Why not a politburo of divinities? From a purely phenomenological standpoint, before the process of internalization and abstraction begins, the world would naturally seem to be filled with a plurality of gods and demons. It is not hard to understand how early man could embrace primitive animism. Things both good and bad happen to us in a bewildering continuity of events. What could seem more natural than to attribute good fortune to gods on our side and to attribute bad fortune to demonic beings that are against us?

An amazing example of a polytheistic description fully congruent with experience comes to mind. Fosdick writes of an East African tribe that had an ingenious explanation of the problem of evil.[3] This tribe believed in a good god who generally kept control of things so that all went well with them. However, things would periodically go wrong as they generally do. When bad or evil things occurred the tribe explained that their god did not want things to go wrong but he had a half-witted brother whom he kept locked up and who, from time to time, escaped. When these escapes occurred, things went from bad to worse. Of course, their god would eventually round up his half-witted brother and then things would be all right until the brother escaped again.

What is fascinating about this explanation of evil is that it is much more coherent with experience than most explanations that Christians give. Furthermore, it can be "verified" empirically. When good things occur the explanation is that God has the brother locked up again and when evil occurs the explanation is that the half-witted brother escaped. But don't worry, God will catch him and lock him up. While this explanation seems absurd to most of us, it is fully congruent with experience.

The ambiguous nature of experience and its multiplicity of positive and negative values lends considerable plausibility to polytheism of some kind. It does not follow that polytheism is true but only that empirically there is something to be said for it.

Whatever polytheistic gods and demons there supposedly were they were clearly not logically necessary, but only further contingent items in the world. Such divinities could not remove the fear of contingency for they were themselves contingent and ambivalent in their attitude towards man. The same situation held for the Greek and Roman gods of antiquity. They, too, were additional contingent items that appeared in the world. They, too, were ambivalent in their attitudes towards man.

In our own time it is interesting to note that James treated polytheism quite seriously and thought that it might well be a live option to consider. We could go on to argue that a residue of polytheism remains in monotheism. After all, what is Satan but a fallen divinity?

In concrete experience, emotional and value qualities are as much a part of the external world as anything else. Concretely, gods and demons have populated the world along with trees and rivers. This is less so now than in the past because we have had centuries of abstraction and internalization which have made modern man's concrete experience appear to be largely devoid of gods and demons. If Jung is right, the process of internalization is only a surface phenomenon and modern man is much closer to primitive man than he likes to think. We may have only given new names to our demons which we fear and dislike such as communism, capitalism, abortionists, anti-abortionists, feminists, racists and etc.

Abstraction from and internalization of much of our concrete experience is essential in order to pursue the concerns of everyday life and science. As this process has unfolded over time, the gods have fled from the center of human consciousness.

Some degree of abstraction may also be essential to make sense of our religious life. To treat everything as having a resident demon is to become victimized by experience rather than to control it. Animism tends to make us powerless before a world of conflicting gods and demons, all working at cross purposes. Pragmatically it became necessary to reduce the number of demons in the world in order to develop a coherent religious life, let alone carry on scientific work. Religiously, the Greek and Roman gods operated more as a kind of supernatural mafia. They had power but little else in terms of ethical and religious sensitivity. To protect themselves, humans had to be sure to be on the right side of the gods or align themselves with one god or goddess.

Logically we find a movement away from animistic pluralism and the gods of Greek and Roman antiquity towards a simpler pluralism of duality as in the forces of good and evil of Zoroastrianism or Manicheism. Indeed, the hypothesis of God and his half-witted brother is a simple form of dualism also, not to mention the residues of dualism in views that speak of God and Satan. I say "residues" here because when we speak of God and Satan, God remains the one supreme Being, whereas in Persian or Manichaean dualism the forces of good and evil are equally divided. Needless to say, nothing has yet been said about necessity in connection with these entities. They all remain contingent.

When we come to the Hebrew God, Jehovah, monotheism is manifest. Satan or pagan gods may exist, but only Jehovah is the supreme Being over all peoples and pagan gods. In Greek mythology Zeus is the chief of the other gods as is Jupiter in Roman mythology; the head position is more like the chairman of a committee or politburo and he does not always get what he wants. In the West with the arrival of the Hebrew God, Jehovah, we reached categorial supremacy and polytheism gave way to monotheism.

In the battle to overcome the insecurities of the contingent world, monotheism is much more religiously rewarding than polytheism. Evil still abounds and gods and demons may still exist, but the world ultimately belongs to Jehovah and his good purposes will win out. As the hymn says, "This is my Father's world." Faith in the ultimate goodness of the universe can be maintained in the face of contingencies that seem to go against such goodness. In polytheism, radical insecurity continues because we never know who or what will win out in the end.

It is also legitimate to speculate that the progression from polytheism to monotheism may be a continuing disclosure of divinity to us as we become ready to accept it. We cannot regard this as a strongly established item of knowledge, however, because of the intrinsic plausibility of polytheism we looked at earlier. Nevertheless, in terms of the requirements of religious adequacy, the option of one supreme Deity seems preferable to the polytheistic option.

When we turn to look at the East, particularly at Hinduism and Buddhism, the trend towards an obvious monotheism is far less apparent. There are clearly monotheistic aspects in both Hinduism and Buddhism but there is much more of a tendency to conjoin this with a multiplicity of polytheistic divinities particularly at the popular level. There is much less tendency in the East to say that we must choose monotheism and reject polytheism. There is also a tendency in the East to accept both good and evil as part of the divine "play" whereas in the West the tendency is to choose good in order to subdue and defeat evil.

In the discussion so far the issue of contingency versus necessity has not appeared. Talk of a supreme Being can also be carried out with no reference to the issue. The issue of divine contingency or necessity became an issue only when some theologians came to the conclusion that to be a supreme Being this Being would also have to exist necessarily. Given the dimensions of evil, and particularly the mass radical evils of modern times, it was felt that a God that simply happened to exist would not be a sufficient basis for a faith that was to remain strong.

When the psalmist says, "Yea, though I walk through the valley of the shadow of death, I shall fear no evil..." and when Job says of Jehovah, "...though He slay me, yet will I trust Him," neither one has an inkling of what contingency and necessity mean to philosophers and theologians. But some theologians maintain that such faith, in the face of all contingencies, can only make sense if God is seen as necessary. Such faith, they feel, would be stupid and irrational if given to another contingent being, who himself might be swallowed up in the flux of the changing world. Later we will reject this theological assumption, but for now this theological viewpoint stresses the deficiencies of a purely contingent God.

No matter how dark things become, the believer must have faith in God's ultimate victory over evil, but it was felt by many theologians that only a necessarily existent God could justify such faith. Whether necessary or contingent, emerging intimations or disclosures of divinity in a monotheistic mode made their appearance in religious thought in both East and West.

A very serious criticism of a purely contingent God centers around what is considered to be an *adequate* object of religious worship. The important issue here is idolatry. All kinds of things have been worshipped in the past, from the physical objects of animism to such things as the sun, the moon and the secular state. Such objects have been worshipped in the past and still are worshipped by some but, by and large, religious persons have come to regard the worship of such contingent objects as acts of idolatry because such objects are unworthy of worship.

These objects are held to be unworthy of worship because it has been increasingly felt that worship should be accorded only to a divine being who is categorically supreme over all other beings. More significantly, the inadequacy of contingent objects resides in their finite nature. Any ordinary contingent object will fail the worshipper in extreme situations of religious need. If things are going well we can worship whatever we please, but if things turn bad a contingent being may well fail to provide spiritual sustenance. There are intrinsic limits to the support that any finite person can give and the state can turn demonic or collapse. The unworthiness of finite objects lies in their intrinsic inadequacy. Religious inadequacy is thought to be a basic feature of contingent beings. Any finite object or set of objects will give out or fail the worshipper at some point. That such failure could even be thought to apply to God is intolerable. Finite objects may be loved, admired and sought after, but to worship finite objects is an act of idolatry.

Adequacy seems to require that any kind of prayer or meditation practices be able to be understood and responded to by divinity; believers must feel secure that whatever form of worship they engage in will not baffle or confound divinity. For religious adequacy to be present, worshippers must not be able to surpass and overcome the "object" of worship and meditation. The sun is inadequate because any act of consciousness already surpasses the sun which has no consciousness. The sun may be bigger and hotter but this is irrelevant in the context of worship.[4]

If we examine any inanimate object, there will be at least one religious way in which persons are superior to that object; persons are consciously aware and the objects are not. Meditation and prayer require consciousness and meditation and prayer also presuppose that divinity contains consciousness in order to respond to such religious practices. Most religious thinkers conclude that any contingent entity will be an inadequate object of worship because it could conceivably be surpassed by humans either now or in the future. In order that divinity remain categorially supreme, it is generally felt that God must then exist necessarily in order to insure religious adequacy.[5] It is generally felt that only a necessarily existent being could remain, in principle, superior to all worshippers.

In situations where God fails to answer prayers or where religious worship fails to provide the support expected and hoped for, the believer is expected to attribute such failure to his own inadequacies and deficiencies and not to attribute them to God. More is involved here than simply paying compliments to God. If the failure is thought to derive from God, religious faith is rendered pointless. Religious adequacy seems to demand that whatever failure may occur must never be attributed to the supreme Being. If God were contingent, failure on God's part would be possible. That such a possibility might occur would seem to doom religious faith. Thus, for many, logical necessity of divine existence seems required to support the needs of religious faith. This requirement is much more stringent than the demand for psychological certainty. Given logical certainty, God would have to exist just as two plus two must be four. If God, in fact, exists contingently, we must admit that it is logically conceivable that there be no God. To admit this would be self-contradictory according to Anselm's followers. Far from being self-contradictory, the non-existence of God is logically possible; there may be no divinity whatsoever. Agnosticism is clearly a plausible position.

If God existed necessarily, agnosticism would not be a plausible position and the believing act of faith would be rendered pointless. There would be only two options. Either God would exist necessarily and His non-existence would be self-contradictory and impossible, or His existence would be logically impossible and His necessary existence would be self-contradictory. Agnosticism leaves the question of God's existence undecided, His existence being a possibility or His non-existence being a possibility. For agnosticism there is no way to decide the issue. To open divine existence to possibility would make God contingent, which is the position I take.

Atheism is an implausible position because it could only hold under two conditions. The first would be that the concept of God is self-contradictory and thus, His existence is impossible, a position which is highly implausible. Under the second condition we would have to know that there is no God, and experience could never justify such a negative existential assertion.

J. N. Findlay has taken the position that the concept of a supreme necessary being is self-contradictory and that, therefore, atheism is a logically necessary conclusion.[6] All a priori approaches to the question of God's existence involve a too easy linguistic sleight of hand as well as failing to come to grips with the realities of religious consciousness. Such approaches seem artificially contrived to make a point.

Empirically theism, pantheism, panentheism and agnosticism seem real possibilities; agnosticism appears to be the most defensible position because it only claims to have no such knowledge on these matters.

Given the nature of our world as we experience it, including the continuous developments of natural science, a world devoid of divinity is a distinct possibility. Whatever the nature of divinity or God may be, divine existence is far from obvious. We generally have to make some effort to believe in God while no such effort is required to believe in chairs, tables and other persons. While I do not think the world is devoid of divinity, to deny the possibility would be erroneous. We have so little hard knowledge about God. Naturalism is a viable and healthy metaphysical position, whether one agrees with it or not.

Epistemologically, divinity is apprehended by us through a series of intimations that we take as pointing towards a being which remains largely hidden from us. Religiously and existentially in the life of man, such intimations have to be supplemented by faith and worship involving revelation as disclosure if the religious life is to be viable. Religious faith may be more fruitfully seen as being analogous to falling in love. If this is so, faith is not something you can talk yourself into, but rather a gift of God that one experientially finds to be present. The all too apparent absences of God and the far from obvious nature of divinity remove such divinity from the realm of the logically necessary in spite of the worries raised by certain types of traditional theology.

In the light of the epistemological situation where strong rational justification for religious belief is absent, it is amazing and odd that people the world over make deep commitments to religious faith and engage in worship, but they do. That religious worship occurs at all is a marvel of human consciousness. That religious belief persists through time and in spite of all criticisms suggests the reality of divine presence. The notion of necessity, however, does not fit coherently into the epistemological situation we have sketched.

It will be the thrust of the rest of the book to argue that the requisite uniqueness and categorial distinctness of divinity can be maintained without resort to necessity. If divinity is to remain an empirically grounded concept, we will argue that divinity, too, must be part of the gift of contingency that we receive. We will further have to argue that divine contingency does not compromise the requirements of religious adequacy or the special nature of the divine.

To experience something is to experience it as contingent; something else could have been experienced instead. If divinity or God can be manifested empirically, as many religious mystics and others have thought, then the divine most likely will appear as contingent too because no logical necessity occurs with whatever we experience. Since rational theology has denied this, we must look at the role of revelation and reason.

NOTES

1. See Chapter II.

2. Karl Barth, *Church Dogmatics* (Edinburgh: T. and T. Clark, 1957) Vol II, p. 307.

3. Harry Emerson Fosdick, *As I See Religion* (New York: Harper & Brothers, 1932) pp. 53–54.

4. For further treatment of religious adequacy and divine contingency, see Chapters VIII and IX.

5. This aspect of the issue has been particulary pushed by Hartshorne. See Charles Hartshorne, *The Logic of Perfection* (LaSalle, IL: Open Court Publishing Co., 1962).

6. J. N. Findlay, "Can God's Existence be Disproved?" in Flew and Macintyre, *New Essays in Philosophical Theology* (London: S.C.M. Press, 1955). Findlay's position holds only if you insist on defining God in a way that makes the concept, "God," a self-contradictory one. The a priori approach is artificial and implausible whether one sets out to prove that God exists necessarily or fails to exist necessarily. Our whole point is that the existence question is an empirical one.

CHAPTER VI
THE ROLE OF REVELATION AND REASON

As we have already seen, everything in the world is contingent. Whether divinity is contingent or not is a matter of dispute. Viewed exclusively in empirical terms, divinity, too, would seem to be another contingent entity in the world but, as we have seen in the previous chapter, to take divinity only as another thing in the world would, phenomenologically, destroy its divine character and also falsely describe our experience.

In order to maintain divine uniqueness it has been felt necessary to leave the realm of experience and resort to revelation and reason. Thus, we must examine the role of revelation and reason in order to see how the tradition attempts to get an adequate concept of divinity.

We will examine how revelation and reason work together in developing what is hopefully a coherent theology. Reason is a tool which can be used in any enterprise while, for Scholastics, revelation rests ultimately on doctrines accepted on the basis of authority. Many theologians claim that the only authority involved in revelation is the internal testimony of the Holy Spirit. It is the faith rather than any doctrine that is authoritative. Whatever authority doctrine has is dependent on the faith disclosure of the Holy Spirit. Nevertheless, viewed from a purely philosophical perspective, when faith is expressed propositionally, we come upon claims that are held to be beyond the bounds of philosophical discussion.

We will also examine the problem of separating true revelations from false ones. We will be talking about revelation in a purely religious sense. Revelation will refer to purported insights about the nature of divinity and what divinity requires of us. We will not be talking about revelation involving sudden insights into empirical matters of fact such as, "I now see that he was a crook all along. It just came over me."

From a purely empirical standpoint we must rely on reports of mystics and prophets in all religious traditions plus the wealth of occurrences of divine impingement on many ordinary persons who are not mystics. These reports contain a great deal of variety and are expressed in terms of culturally conditioned religious categories. For example, Buddhist and Christian theologies differ so the reports will differ too. In spite of this, there are certain threads of similarity that run through the reports of many mystics. As William James said of the mystic who feels his consciousness merge with a larger consciousness, "He becomes conscious that this higher part is conterminous and continuous with a *more* of the same quality, which is operative in the universe outside of him..."[1] This larger center of consciousness I am calling divinity. James's description has the flavor of Hindu and Buddhist descriptions in stressing the merging of one consciousness into a larger consciousness. However, his phenomenological description is easily adaptable to include the I-Thou type of encounter where God and man remain distinct entities.

James's description is deliberately kept vague in order to identify a common thread which runs through the descriptions of divinity that occur in different religious traditions. Empirically, mystical experiences have occurred and continue to occur. What characterizes such experiences is the feeling that one comes up against a larger center of consciousness, external to the self or to society. Taken in its simplest terms such an encounter would be contingent because whatever we come up against in experience need not have appeared at all; it just happens.

It should be kept in mind that most believers are not mystics and that mysticism is not a common phenomenon. Mystical experience is important, however, because it manifests the most dramatic form of divine impingement on human consciousness and can be a useful paradigm when considering empirical aspects of divinity.

Mystical experiences are the most obvious types of experience manifesting divinity, but other more subtle and commonplace experiences seem to point to divinity too.[2] Empirically we cannot get very specific. We have a religious gift of experience or set of experiences with an apparent larger consciousness that exceeds the self or society.

To argue that we have arrived at a personal God, however, goes beyond the common element that is presented empirically. What we experience directly are vague but often powerful numinous impingements which are described in detail by the mystics. When we designate a personal God as the source of these experiences, we are putting an interpretation on them which goes beyond what is immediately given. Experience itself remains at a vague suggestive level. Empirically the common element discloses intimations of divinity.

In order to flesh out such intimations in terms of what is believed by a religious community, recourse is made to revelation. Taking off from a given disclosure, theology brings the tool of reason to bear in order to develop coherent and persuasive doctrines of divinity or God. That this should occur is natural and understandable. While all experience is grist for the mill, in order to be useful all experience gets interpreted in various ways in everyday life and in science. Revelation and reason are the tools of interpretation of religious phenomena. Without interpretation nothing could be known or accomplished.

What must be kept in mind, however, is that in the process of interpretation one goes beyond experience, strictly speaking, by taking it in a certain way. In other words, experience never really occurs without some interpretation being put upon it. Even James's characterization of mystical experience as impingement on us by a larger consciousness is interpretive to some degree. He tries to remain as close to the pure experience as possible but cannot avoid some interpretive framework, particularly if he is going to talk about it. As we saw earlier, only Zen Buddhists radically attempt to avoid all interpretation of experience but can only do so by remaining silent, which they do not always succeed in doing.

Usually, to interpret religious experience the prophet or religious leader explains his experience as a revelation from the divine dimension in general or from God in particular, depending on whose revelation is being talked about. We call it revelation because the "word of God" is presumably revealed to a human being or beings and is then interpreted to the religious followers as being the word of God or some other kind of divine disclosure. Such revelation can be transmitted directly to a prophet who then proclaims it verbally to the multitude, or it can get enshrined in a written document such as the Bible, which is then taken to be the revealed word of God.

While much of our concern will be with revelation as expressed in propositions involving truth claims, revelation occurs to people first of all in *events* seen as having deep religious import. Events get talked about eventually and theological propositions get formulated about the meaning of these events, but, first of all, the events have to be seen by a religious community as revealing the divine.

Moses leading the Jews out of Egypt is one of the most significant religiously impregnated events for the Jewish community. Empirically we see a deeply religious community achieving freedom from an oppressor. There are many similar events throughout history. The Jews see the direct care of God for His chosen people in the act of liberation from Egypt. The "long march" from Egypt to freedom led by Moses reveals the direction and love of God for His people. For Jews, it is primarily a deeply significant event of divine disclosure celebrated to this day. "The long march" of the Chinese

Communists in the nineteen thirties under Mao Tse Tung, on the other hand, had deep political significance for the Chinese Communists but no type of divine disclosure was involved.

Divine revelation or disclosure is not always positive for a religious community. The military defeats that the Israelites suffered were taken as events where divine wrath and displeasure were displayed towards His wayward people.

Consider the significance of the resurrection for orthodox Christians. This event is at the heart of the Christian revelation. Many have argued with considerable plausibility that if things had ended with the crucifixion, there would be no Christian religion today. Empirically, it is highly doubtful that a literal resurrection ever occurred. Religiously, the resurrection denotes an event of radical divine disclosure, a disclosure of the presence of Christ to his followers. For most believers the term "resurrection" is not used metaphorically. Regardless of what empirically may or may not have happened, *phenomenologically*, the presence of the living God was felt by the disciples after the crucifixion. On the basis of the revelation event the disciples felt strongly that the crucifixion was not the end of the Christian saga but only the beginning.

It is difficult to deal with an event revelation like the resurrection in empirical terms. At the empirical level we can only talk in terms of the psychological impact that Jesus had on the disciples. The impact of the personality of Jesus on his followers was of unusual intensity even for a religious leader. We should be in no doubt, however, that at the phenomenological level Christ rose from the dead as far as the disciples were concerned and that event has become the keystone of the whole body of Christian revelation. Without the resurrection Jesus becomes another failed though sublime religious leader. With the resurrection, belief in Jesus's entire life and teaching is "perceived" as God becoming man and the entire Christian corpus developed from that.

A revelation event is a public event in that it is shared by a religious community of faith, but it is clearly not a public event in the ordinary sense in which we use the term. The death of Caesar is a public event in the latter sense. Outside the bounds of a given religious community of faith, the revelation event is either totally delusory or else an event that can be given a straightforward, empirical interpretation. The crucifixion was a public event in the obvious sense but the resurrection was not.

Judaism has a strong prophetic tradition for the transmission of revelation, whereas Protestantism, in varying degrees, tends to take the life of Jesus and the Bible to be the revealed Word of God. For Catholics, the revealed Word of God is transmitted also by the Church tradition expressed through various pronouncements down through the ages.

When we speak of revelation we are not speaking of every kind of revelation that some individual or other feels is the Word of God. All kinds of people have claimed to have messages from God, but taken together such reports form a chaotic and contradictory mass.

When dealing with conflicting revelations we are faced with a deep epistemic scandal because there is really no way to decide which are sound revelations and which are not. All revelations ultimately appeal to the authority of those who disclose them to the followers. But the element of epistemic scandal can be reduced. The method is to reduce the chaotic mass of individual revelations by subjecting them to the scrutiny of a religious community. The community will reject many claims as spurious and accept others as valid, and though the appeal remains ultimately to authority, there is at least a quasi public aspect to such procedures. The chaos of conflicting claims gets reduced considerably.

Another factor in judging the validity of a revelation is the test of time. We are faced today, as in times past, with the phenomenon of instant groups or cults. Many of these come and go and are so far out as to defy simple common sense and ethics. The recent Jim Jones cult is a case in point as are the "Moonies." The importance of a long historical tradition cannot be overemphasized. In the process of centuries, many absurdities get rooted out. It is true that a long historical tradition like that of the Catholic Church can become dogmatic and authoritarian and freeze out new emerging religious insights as heretical. Nevertheless, the Catholic Church has an impressive history of religious saintliness and insight over the centuries. It has developed procedures and methods for trying to validate genuine revelation from spurious claims to revelation. Although these procedures are epistemically questionable, they do call on the collective wisdom of the Church over time and bring about as much public check as one can to the area of revelation. Whether the Roman Catholic Curia's control allowed for sufficient public check as is desirable was a matter of dispute and became a primary Reformation issue. In terms of validating revelations, what is true of Catholics is also true, in varying degrees, of Buddhists, Hindus, Protestants, Moslems and Jews.

In all these cases the epistemic scandal of revelation is reduced, if not eliminated. In the end we are still dependent on the appeal to authority, but the authority is checked by various procedures of one kind or another. Revealed events and theological pronouncements deserve serious consideration when they emerge from an historical tradition that has lasted over a considerable period of time.

Revelation is essentially a *social* manifestation of religion. A solitary prophet may have what he or she takes to be a message from God, but it doesn't really become a revelation until the solitary prophet has followers who take his pronouncements to be a message from divinity and the message becomes part of a corporate historical tradition. This account is oversimplified to bring out the logic of revelation. One doesn't usually start out as a solitary being, collect followers and then propound a revelation to them although this has been done. Usually, what we find are existent religious communities, already operating as social institutions, propounding doctrines that for centuries have been held as revealed truths of particular religions. Whether the individual or the group came first is like the question of the chicken or the egg. What we find empirically are new revelations that are introduced into already existent religious institutions. Into this context a new revelation appears to supplement or extend already established revealed doctrines. While a new religion may have started with the revealed doctrine of an individual such as Buddha or Christ, Buddhism arose in the context of an already existent Hinduism and Christianty arose out of an already existent Judaism.

The point is that so-called revealed truths are part of the network of an organized, social, religious institution. While such revealed truths hopefully are based on the empirical aspects of divinity we spoke of earlier, as truths that we are supposed to adhere to they are presented to us in a non-empirical manner. We are basically asked to accept revealed truths on the basis of what theologians tell us rests on the inner testimony of the holy spirit and *not* on a blatant appeal to authority. However, for the non-believer, outside the lifeworld of faith, the basic faith commitment is not subject to question or rejection on the basis of philosophical criticism.

A revelation may contain empirical components, such as a divine injunction to engage in or refrain from certain practices. The only justification for regarding any of these empirical components as commandments of God, however, is that the particular religious institution propounding them or an emerging new prophet says they are. To question a revelation evidences a lack of faith. Many particular revelations lack any empirical component altogether such as the Christian doctrine of the Trinity.

If revealed doctrines had no basis in the empirical disclosures of divinity we talked of earlier, we could dismiss them as being various species of wish-fulfillment with no basis in external reality. However, the massive reports of the mystics and other religious seers over time make such dismissal inappropriate. Revealed doctrines need to be taken seriously as clues or interpretations of the divine which disclose themselves in experience.

There are various clues to the divine that we can find in revealed doctrines, provided we interpret cautiously. The symbolism of the cross involved in the death and resurrection of Christ can be taken as an indication that God involves Himself with us in our sufferings and indeed undergoes our experiences with us. The experiences that are undergone by man appear to be participated in and known by God in a direct feeling way, not simply as a detatched, intellectual awareness. The Ten Commandments of the Old Testament and the moral injunctions given by Jesus in the New Testament, though taken as revealed truths, can also be seen as clues to the moral disclosures of divinity.

Revealed truths are belief based doctrines propounded by a religious institution. In institutional religion such revelations are not to be taken as clues to the divine but rather as basic truths which rest ultimately on faith commitment. It is true that theology may involve radical questioning concerning issues regarding faith but, no matter how interpreted, the basic revelation is to be accepted in faith and supported by the religious community. To rely ultimately *only* on truths that are accepted on authority is to cut the ties to the empirical roots which constitute the life-blood of the religious life. Avoiding the pitfalls of revealed dogma taken on faith while maintaining the insights of revelation disclosed by the fluid and changing empirical aspects of religion is a difficult task.

Quakerism presents an interesting and unique case study in trying to stay close to the empirical disclosures of divinity, on the one hand, while retaining some group religious stability on the other. Quakers, historically and in the present, are very radical in rejecting revealed truths as a body of doctrine that should be written down and to which the members of the meeting are expected to conform. Through most of their history they also rejected a paid ministry as an intermediary between the congregation and God. In a unique form of Protestantism, Quakers argue that the individual can relate to God directly without the intermediary of a paid ministry.

Although they believe in group religious practices, Quaker practice consists of a silent unprogrammed meeting for worship instead of a church service. Out of the silent meeting, individuals may speak but only as they feel themselves directed by God. Such revelations as occur will come out of the silent meetings for worship.

It is particularly important that a person not speak in meeting just because he has something he wants to say. Quakers should sit in silence unless and until one of them feels an overwhelming urge to deliver a message. In such a situation, it is felt, God will deliver his insights through the speaker at times of God's own choosing. Quakers are so insistent on this point that in times past they sometimes attempted to speak without controlling their speech mechanisms, because to do so would mean that the speaker was getting in the way and distorting the divine message. This led to what was called a "sing-song" method of delivery where the speaker was only to be a transmission device for divine disclosure. The author can remember as a small boy, hearing this kind of delivery in meeting. Its effect was so odd, however, that the method was given up, for, ironically, all it did was draw attention *to* the speaker instead of away from him. The idea behind speaking in meeting remains intact, however, no matter how often it may be violated in practice.

With no codified corporate confession of faith as guideline and with various divinely inspired messages coming out of the meeting, this would seem to allow for a situation approaching anarchy in which it would be very difficult for a religious group to function coherently. Quakers are realistic enough, however, to realize that in spite of everything, since humans transmit the message, it does not follow that all messages come from God or that, if they do, they are not distorted in transmittal.

Like all religious groups, Quakers face the problem of trying to distinguish between a genuine revelation from God and a spurious one. Other groups have a body of revealed doctrine, already taken as divine disclosure, against which to measure claims to new divine disclosure. Who speaks with an authoritative voice within Quakerism? There is no appeal to authority in the sense of a sacred written corporate code that must be adhered to. There is a written body of "faith and practice" and various Quaker "testimonies" that represent collective Quaker insight over the years, but such writings serve only as guidelines for Quaker practice and do not represent any body of doctrine that must be conformed to. In the meeting for worship all members are equal before God but, in fact, as in the case with other groups, "Some are more equal than others."

In any group there are individuals who stand out as leaders and to whom the group turns for guidance and advice. These are individuals who naturally rise to the top, who are respected by the whole group. The informal Quaker term for such leaders is "weighty Friends." These are the people who tend to carry more weight in the meeting than others, those to whom everyone listens carefully when they speak. A weighty Friend functions as "one who speaks with authority and not as the scribes."

While there is a certain amount of jocularity about who is and who isn't a weighty Friend, the term is not meant to designate those persons who are rather pompous or who speak in meeting much more than they should. When weighty Friends express their concerns, the meeting listens with special attention because they feel that through such persons God discloses himself. There is no public method of certifying who is a weighty Friend, nor does it follow that God can disclose himself only through weighty Friends.

When anyone speaks or expresses a "concern," the message must pass the test of the "sense of the meeting," of which we will have more to say shortly. The sense of the meeting is not required whenever anyone speaks in meeting. When most messages are delivered they are either accepted or not accepted by the worshippers in the silence that follows. It is when someone expresses a "concern" that calls for some group action or response that the sense of the meeting is invoked.

There is no sure method for testing whether a revelation is genuine or not, whether one is speaking of Quakers or non-Quakers. What the silent meeting does do is attempt to keep the members as close as possible to the disclosures of God, as they may occur, rather than interpose a stated creedal doctrine or priestly interpretation between the believer and the disclosure. The Quaker argument against the traditional paid ministry of other churches is that there is no guarantee that the paid minister or priest is any closer to God than anyone else just because he has studied for this position and is paid. In some denominations frequently priests and ministers are appointed by the church beaurocracy and, thus, are apt to represent the interests of that bureaucracy. Obviously this is not always so for there have always been priests and ministers of outstanding spiritual depth and leadership. However, there is a danger that reliance on a professional group for spiritual leadership will lead to the decline of the church, to increased reliance on frozen dogma and a more or less passive laity that will accept on authority whatever the paid spiritual professionals say.

The history of both Catholic and Protestant churches supplies much data for such worries. The paid professional also tends to bypass the more direct Quaker method of gaining leadership through the sense of the meeting itself. Does this mean that Quakers are less prone to religious ossification and static resistance to new growth than other churches? Unfortunately, no. Stale bureaucratic procedures affect Quakerism just as they do other groups. In early Quakerism the "plain language" of "thee" and "thou" was introduced so that Quakers could give testimony that all men, including kings, should be addressed as equals before God. Today this quaint custom, where it survives, ironically tends to have precisely the opposite effect from what was intended. The use of "plain language" tends to set Quakers apart from others, as though they were some special "in" group. This may not be felt by Quakers and is not intended, but it is felt by non-Quakers in a mixed group.

The problem of "Who speaks with authority?" is difficult in any case, and, epistemologically, neither Quakers nor members of any other religious group can come up with plausible or rational criteria that will certify that a particular utterance is a disclosure from God. In general, churches take a dim view of new claims to divine revelation that arise. We can't really justify every claim that someone makes that he has spoken with God or received a new message from Him.

In the absence of any sound rational method of separating true claims from false ones, what is generally done is that a religious institution measures such claims against an already established body of creedal belief. If the claim fails the test of complying with such creeds, it is rejected. If the claim passes the test of dogma, the character and soundness of the person making the claim still has to be sharply looked at. Immediate acceptance of such claims is rejected because careful validation procedures take time and also because time itself is a partial determining factor as to whether such claims are substantial or merely a passing fancy.

No matter how elaborate the procedures for testing revelation claims which all religious institutions face, the proposed validation is no stronger than the creeds appealed to which are already based on faith. Nevertheless, it is hard to see what else could be done. A given claim to divine insight must at least be measured against the religious group experience which may extend back over many centuries.

Returning to the Quaker meeting for worship, the messages given in meeting must be taken in the spirit in which they were given. If, however, any line of action or procedure seems called for, the message becomes a Quaker "concern" and for the concern to be considered a genuine "leading" from God it must be accepted by the group as the sense of the meeting. Here a fascinating and profound checking procedure arises which avoids the anarchy of all present going off on their own revelation and at the same time tries to test whether the particular concern is a genuine revelation from God.

All Quaker business is conducted by appealing to the sense of the meeting. To obtain this, no voting method is used. Friends sit in silence, speaking only as they "feel led" to speak to the concern. If a general assent seems to arise out of the meeting, the clerk will declare that a sense of the meeting has been achieved and that the concern is a genuine one, revealed by God. General assent is usually manifested by various members saying in the meeting, "I approve" of the proposal or action under consideration. If, on the other hand, there is hesitancy or resistance on the part of some, or possibly only *one*, then the matter is put off until it can be accepted with "clearness." The assumption of the whole procedure is that the group is genuinely interested in the will of God and that out of the silence, the will of God will emerge in the sense of the meeting. If hesitancy is expressed about the concern it is thought likely that God's will is not being manifested. There is no assumption that majority rule is necessarily the will of God, so voting will not do. The divine will could conceivably be expressed by one lone cantankerous individual whose view may or may not ultimately become the sense of the meeting. We cannot pre-judge the question of whom God chooses to speak through.

I cite Quakerism here because it represents a very interesting attempt to find out what a genuine revelation of God might be, by relying on the procedures of silent worship rather than on a codified revealed church doctrine. There is nothing infallible about such a procedure and since Quakers are no better or worse than anyone else, the method is and has been subject to abuse. Ego and struggle for power can operate here just as it does elsewhere. If individual power plays are all that is involved, the method would fail entirely. Also, given the amount of self-deception and mixed motives involved in decision-making processes, the method probably fails more frequently than is recognized.

The astonishing thing is that it ever leads to consensus at all. And when it works, as it frequently does, it can only work because the members of the group are honestly trying, "out of the silence," to find the will of God rather than their own will. There is nothing certain about this group check. Who knows whether the will of God has really been expressed? From an empiricist perspective it is an interesting method of procedure and, given intimations of divinity, is just as likely to express divine leadings as reliance on written creeds and dogmas or free response to the incarnate Word of God that other religious groups propound. The method also allows for a continuing and open expression of God's will. For Quakers as well as others, the will of the most dominant and charismatic members may prevail rather than the will of God and there is no sure method to tell which. All the believer can do is reside in the faith that God can manifest His influence in a multiplicity of ways. The best that can be done is to maintain religious communities which discourage egoism and allow channels for divine leading.

While Quakerism presents an instructive case study in one way to evaluate revealed truths, in practice its institutional expression is often not that different from other churches. Historically it was, and basically still is, a Christian body. The founder, George Fox, maintained strongly, "There is one, even Christ Jesus, that can speak to thy condition."[3]

An accretion of Quaker practices occurs over time. The peace testimony represents one such accretion. Quaker pacifism as an expression of divine revealed insight is well known to the world and, indeed, continues to provide its healing influence on the struggles of mankind.

What is not so well known but needs stressing is that pacifism, while an integral part of historical Quakerism, has never been and is not now a dogma or creedal requirement to which all Quakers must subscribe. Many Quakers in good standing are not pacifists and have served in the armed forces. Pacifism is a testimony that historical Quakerism hopes all Quakers and, indeed, all mankind will eventually accept. But in the meantime, every person must follow his or her own conscience in the matter. When William Penn, who had been a military man, asked George Fox if he had to leave the military to become a Quaker, Fox replied, "Wear thy sword as long as thou canst."[4] What this is generally interpreted to mean is that Penn was to stay in the military until he felt a clear call from God that he should not.

Again we see that while there is a group check or attempted consensus in the sense of the meeting concerning God's revelation, in the last analysis an individual confronts God with her own conscience. While conscience plays an important role in other Christian groups, when push comes to shove the creedal requirements of written revelation in a historical tradition generally determine what is acceptable behavior for a member of the group.

Even being a Christian is not necessarily a Quaker requirement today. It depends on which Quaker group you belong to. It would be more accurate to speak of multiple Quakerisms rather than a single Quakerism. In the last century a sizeable group of American Quakers gave up the silent meeting altogether, opting for a paid ministry and churches like other Christian groups. Those who call themselves Quakers run the gamut from Biblical fundamentalists to universalistic pantheists.

Generally, a written and codified revelation is accepted by a religious community which already takes it as fact. Unless the religious community is renewed by new mystical experiences, and such renewal usually happens, the institution becomes ossified in dogma which is transmitted in an authoritarian manner to the followers. All human institutions tend to become ossified in bureaucratic procedures which then perpetuate themselves; religious institutions are no exception. Religious history shows a constant struggle between the mystics or prophets and the bureaucrats. It seems to take a profoundly sensitive temperament to transmit a revelation by founding a religion. Such a person generally does not have the type of temperament to organize and perpetuate a church institution. Jesus was the original source of revelation for Christianity, but it took an organizing mind like Paul's to set the church on its path as an institution. The two types are not mutually exclusive, for Paul had first-hand religious experience, but his main genius was in organization.

Revelation presents a particularly thorny problem for philosophy. Because of its appeal to authority, revelation places itself outside the context of philosophical debate where reason and experience are relied on to settle issues. Of course, revelation uses reason to substantiate its position in theology, but ultimately, in theology, the critic comes up against certain beliefs about God and the world which are not open to debate or question. Anyone who has studied medieval philosophy is aware of the struggle between faith and reason. A major source of embarrassment in revelation is what to do when reason arrives at conclusions about God that conflict with what revelation requires one to believe.

From an empiricist perspective revelation is a non-rational intrusion propounding "truths" without empirical support. Empirically, Jesus was a man and a profound religious teacher, much like other religious leaders, though admittedly unusual and forceful. Others have healed the sick and preached doctrines of divinity and human salvation. The assertion that Jesus is uniquely and exclusively divine, being God incarnated in the Son, has no empirical warrant whatsoever. The critic is given no choice but to hope this is true on the basis of faith or to reject it or leave it undecided. The case is similar to other revealed doctrines. Empirically we have seen that divinity manifests itself at least on the phenomenological level. But there is no way that empirically we could come to the conclusion that God is trinitarian in nature. St. Thomas and other church fathers acknowledged and accepted the division between revelation and experience. Thomas and others hoped to incorporate reason and revelation into a coherent theology with revelation remaining ultimately supreme and unquestioned.

Within the Christian faith the hope is that reason and revelation "can lie down together," though just how this is to be done has been a matter of continuous dispute within the church. Both inside and outside the context of the organized church there is no resolution. Philosophy based on experience finds truths that conflict with revealed doctrines. We must come back to revelation shortly and see if there is not a more positive way of looking at it, but the difficulties are real and must be dealt with. Let us turn for a moment to the role of reason.

Experience of any kind is already impregnated by reason and religious experience is no exception. The use of the term, "God," is one way for reason to more precisely categorize the vague empirical presentations of divinity we looked at earlier. The fact that the term, "God," may be derived through the help of reason does not make God a non-empirical creature of reason's invention. As we shall see shortly, the term, "God," is grounded in religious experience, but the use of the term involves an interpretive component which takes us beyond a vague larger consciousness.

Since all experience involves rational interpretation, religious experience is not necessarily compromised by such interpretation. It depends on how it is done. If done well, reason can enrich our description and comprehension of experience. If done badly, reason can make our experience seem unintelligible. Reason is excessive if it engages in speculation that has no relation to religious experience.

Some strains of orthodox Christian revelation, through the use of reason, maintain that anyone who thinks it is possible that God doesn't exist doesn't know what he or she is talking about. Such views contend that the agnostic and the atheist are not only wrong but their error is due to a basic conceptual confusion. As Anselm said centuries ago, "The fool hath said in his heart, there is no God."[5] Just as only an idiot could think that a round object could also be square, so only one who failed to think through the concept of God could think that God could fail to exist. Anyone who possesses adequate knowledge knows that a round object is necessarily not a square object. In a similar way anyone who has thought through the idea of God knows His existence is necessary.

Revelation doesn't usually state the issue in these clear logical terms. Revelation says God, as the supreme Being, is eternal and everlasting, the be-all and end-all of everything that is. Belief in God's reality is an essential requirement of faith and doubt is evidence of weakness of faith. Reason backs up revelation at this point by saying that God's non-existence is literally inconceivable just as a round square is inconceivable. The agnostic, the atheist and the naturalist are simply confused about the correct usage of the term, "God."

If revelation and reason were correct on this point, disagreement would be based only on a confusion about how the term, "God," is to be used. Once the confusion is cleared up, there would be far fewer agnostics, atheists and naturalists. In fact, once the confusion is cleared up, there should be *no* atheists, agnostics and naturalists. But the facts are otherwise. Leaving aside the doubts about God engendered by the terrible events mankind has lived through in our century, the belief that divinity manifests itself at all is far from self-evident or logically certain. Even as a child, we learn early about "sealing wax and cabbages and kings," but God remains one of the most peculiar entities presented to us for our acceptance. True enough, there are intimations of divinity in experience, but the full-fledged divine being of Jewish and Christian faith is, indeed, a hidden God. I am not saying there couldn't be such a God. I am saying that belief in such a God is open to very reasonable doubt even after one has worked through the ontological argument. After working through the argument for God's necessity, both "the fool" and the wise man may remain in existential anguish about God's reality. Thus, the combination of revelation and reason, which wants to make God's existence a logical certainty, is wrong.

What revelation can do is to give a sense of stability and continuity to a religious community. The desire for psychological certainty can be satisfied by belief in a set of doctrines which are taken to be true on the basis of faith in the revelation. Few people are able to function on their own religiously, due to the elusive and ambiguous manifestations of divinity. Most, following the lead of saints and mystics, depend on a stable and reasonably coherent set of beliefs, propounded and accepted in a social setting with others. Direct religious experience of divinity comes and goes and is fraught with ambiguity, leading to multiple interpretations. A set of revealed truths, unchanging and continuous, supported by a believing community, encourages those with faith to have a bed-rock certainty and stability about God on which they can rely.

Whatever we may think of religious institutions, it is hard to see how they could be built and maintained by relying exclusively on the vague hints and intimations of divinity that experience provides.

Written revealed creeds not only provide continuity and stability to a church, they can also allow us to flesh out doctrines of divinity or God. In spite of inadequacies in the traditional Judeo-Christian concept of God, revealed truths about God bring out strongly the aspect of God as personal in nature. This is a crucial feature when dealing with the religious adequacy of the object of worship.

While some revealed doctrines about God tend to get cast in stone and become dogmatically followed, the history of revealed doctrine can be seen as a kind of testing ground for various concepts of divinity. At best they represent real insights into the nature of divinity. Those who are sensitively attuned to disclosure of the divine forge ahead and break new ground. The rest of us may follow in their footsteps, not in their experience necessarily, but at least in their beliefs. For example, following the lead of mystics and saints, religious communities have moved slowly from seeing God as belonging exclusively to one group to seeing God as concerned equally with all creatures, the non-human as well as the human. Religious communities have moved slowly from seeing God exclusively in terms of a political power model to seeing God as a persuasive force of love.

Some would argue that one of these emerging insights is to see God as necessary rather than contingent. The thrust of this study is that God is not necessary. But am I not simply stressing personal preference here? Why assume that the qualities of divinity I favor provide us genuine insight and the qualities I do not favor do not? I cannot deny that personal preference is operative here. All I can ask readers to do is to compare their own insights and intimations with those I present and try to see which seem more plausible. Given my preference for empirical disclosure, all such disclosures would have to be of contingent entities, whether of divinity or anything else. All we can do is attempt to devise a coherent over-all view that takes full account of our religious life. Outside the "circle of faith," revelation cannot make a case for anything by simply asserting that it is revealed to be so by the church, scripture or God Himself.

When we turn to reason, we see that it is a tool that can be widely used. As used in theology, it helps support and sustain theological conclusions which, as we have seen, are ultimately grounded in revelation. Eventually we are driven back to certain propositions and beliefs which are not subject to question and debate. In the interim, however, a great deal of theological argument and debate occurs. Reason is the tool that knits the findings of revelation together in what is hopefully a coherent and plausible theology.

Reason is a useful tool in natural theology and philosophy of religion. Natural theology purports to draw conclusions about God by looking at the natural world rather than by specific reliance on revelation. However, natural theology has a special agenda in that every kind of theology is designed to support a particular organized religious viewpoint. We can only have a specific theology such as Lutheran, Catholic or Baptist, not theology in general. What natural theology tries to do is see what we can say about God by relying on empirical and rational argument alone, but natural theology must be supplemented by appeal to revealed theology to provide an adequate overall theological viewpoint. The legitimate and recognized purpose of any theology is to justify the revealed doctrines of a particular religious community. For theology, reason is a tool to help us explain doctrines and beliefs that ultimately rest on faith in a particular revelation.

When we come to philosophy of religion, we are studying religion as a phenomenon, setting aside any previous beliefs in revealed truths we may have, relying on reason and experience exclusively. Our study is obviously in philosophy of religion, not theology. We look at religion philosophically just as we might look at science or politics philosophically. Revelation and its accompanying belief affect one's whole life orientation. A person so touched by divinity is analogous to a person who has fallen in love. Religious faith, like falling in love, is a concrete emotional response to "something" apprehended. Philosophy involves an abstract discussion of such phenomena. This is why we cannot have recourse to revelation as a legitimate method of establishing conclusions in this study.

As we saw in Chapter V, reason can be used as a tool to support revealed doctrine. Some revealed Christian doctrines take God to exist necessarily and not contingently; we have seen how reason arrives at that conclusion. But reason itself is neutral. As a tool it can be used to argue for either a contingent or a necessary God. Reason, like revelation, can also be used to help develop a religiously adequate doctrine of God. This development process can either occur in theology or philosophy of religion. As has been indicated, in order to maintain that divinity has a special and unique designation we usually turn to revelation and reason. Revelation does this by declaring God's unique superiority to everything else to be a matter of faith. Reason seeks to support divine uniqueness by arguing for God's necessary existence. Our empiricist approach does not allow us to resort to either of these strategies. We, too, want to maintain divine uniqueness while holding on to divine contingency. How this might be done will be examined in a later chapter.[6]

NOTES

1. William James, *The Varieties of Religious Experience* (New York: Longmans, Green and Co., 1935) p. 508.

2. See my *Intimations of Divinity* (New York: Peter Lang Publishing Co., Chapter 9, 1989).

3. *The Journal of George Fox* (New York: E.P. Dutton and Co., 1924) p. 8.

4. William I. Hull, *William Penn: A Topical Biography* (London: Oxford University Press, 1937) p. 308.

5. Anselm, *Proslogium* in *St. Anselm — Basic Writings* (La Salle, IL: Open Court Publishing Co., 1962) Chapter II; See also Psalm XIV.

6. See Chapter X.

CHAPTER VII
DIVINE CONTINGENCY AS GIFT

The assumption that contingency must be grounded in some kind of necessary being or rational ground has been made for philosophical and religious reasons. In both cases it was felt that an ironclad foundation was needed to support the philosophical and religious structure. In recent religious and philosophical literature this architectural analogy has been called into question. Philosophical systems and religious faith are not like buildings and houses which require a solid foundation.

Contingency is not a poor relation that must be taken in and supported by some kind of necessary being. In terms of what experience presents us, contingency reigns, no matter how rich a view we take of experience. While much traditional philosophy accepts the ultimate contingency of persons and the world, traditional rationalist philosophy feels that neither world nor persons would exist at all unless both were grounded rationally in either a necessarily divine being or a necessary principle of sufficient reason. The rationalist view has also made inroads into Western theology, but a significant number of theologians believe such an incursion to be unwarranted.

The contingent world can be seen as a gift and experience as the conveyor belt of contingency. There seems to be no ultimate reason why there must be a world or persons must be in the world. Our birth and experiences are gifts which we just find to be the case. They are not always happy gifts, but they are still gifts in the sense that nothing necessitates that they appear in an absolute sense. The simple appearance of things out of the blue is gift-like when viewed in terms of experience. Of course any thing or collection of things in the world, or any person, can only appear in some kind of causal nexus. Contingency does not mean creation ex nihilo as far as the things and persons of the world are concerned taken one at a time. But that there should be any kind of a world at all, including God, rather than nothing, remains an ultimate mystery.

Instead of the rational urge to ground contingency in a necessary being, let us speak of the religious urge for God. Assuming God is apparent at all, the sense of His presence as well as His absence is existential in the fullest sense of that term. God's presence is an existential disclosure because the reality of God is always open to doubt. We must reach out in faith towards God rather than possessing solid knowledge of Him. Since the God question is always open to doubt, the existence status of God would appear to be contingent. Faith combined with doubt is a real factor in the religious strivings of many persons. Faith can manifest itself in the face of objective uncertainty about God as Kierkegaard indicated. If it were clearly apparent that God was a necessary being, such existential doubt would be inexplicable. However, doubt and faith mix naturally in the religious life, contrary to impressions that faith means that everything has to be nailed down tight. Thus, divine contingency would seem to be called for.

Many would deny this implication, pointing out that doubt may only reflect the lack of faith on the part of many persons. Yet in the end, it is really sobering how little we know about the divine component of reality. To assert that divinity is a part of the real at all is quite an assertion and is not strongly supportable in the usual epistemic terms. To go on and assert the necessity of the divine component seems excessive.

What does seem significant and must be taken account of is the fact that many persons have a religious assurance of God's presence which removes all doubts from their minds. The happy assurance that one is loved by another person, although not identical to this religious assurance, is analogous to it. The religious assurance is special and something different. It is this kind of religious faith that some thinkers may have translated into ontological terms as God's necessary existence but the two are as different as night and day. Assurance of the love of God is one thing, but the necessity of God is completely different. The first is an intense psychological and emotional state of religious consciousness related to a real divine, though contingent, component. The other is just an abstract ontological commitment which is designed to back up religious faith in a rational manner.

Religious assurance that some have is indeed a fortunate gift, for it is not a possession of all believers. When it is manifested it is a contingent gift, which is manifested empirically, regardless of the ontological status of divinity.

From a purely religious perspective, I want to suggest that the ontological status of divinity appears to be a purely abstract theoretical issue. It is a concern of theologians and philosophers exclusively. Theologians and philosophers take their data from the actual religious life of devotion and faith. In the life of faith we may talk of the assurance of divine manifestation in terms of the psychological certainty of God's support. Even psychological certainty is not shared by all believers. Some theologians and philosophers, taking psychological certainty as data, translate this into logical certainty and the necessity of the divine.

It is the people with secure and deep faith in a supreme being that we tend to look to for spiritual leadership. Theirs is indeed a "consummation devoutly to be wished," but for large numbers of persons their faith is not this secure and is often subject to constant testing and doubt. To translate the secure faith of the few as requiring the necessity of God's existence is, however, a highly questionable procedure.

Take the optimal case of religious faith, one not characteristic of all believers by any means. By optimal case I mean one where the believer is secure in his faith and where God is constantly felt as present. Such a secure religious faith is not equivalent to knowing with logical certainty that God exists. Logical certainty requires only a purely intellectual or rational competence. A computer can establish logical certainty far quicker than we can. Secure faith is centered around a feeling that God is ultimately dependable, no matter what occurs. The religious feeling is far different from the logical contention that God exists, no matter what occurs. The latter defines a necessary truth. The Anselmians say that the statement, "God exists," is necessarily true no matter what occurs in the empirical world, hence God cannot exist contingently. Even if we accept this logical point, for the moment, it is not required by or equivalent to a secure religious faith of the optimal kind.

A fully developed religious faith points towards an ultimate belief in the moral dependability of God. I say this in spite of Kierkegaard's warning about the danger of identifying our moral concerns with God's will. The danger is a real one but central to God's moral dependability is the emerging insight that living creatures have intrinsic worth in the sight of God. We might say that the person with a fully developed religious faith regards the divine moral dependability as highly predictable, almost lawlike. We are not speaking about lawlike in the scientific sense, but a moral and religious dependability which the man of secure faith has.

For the believer we are considering, there tends to be a sense of uplifting, divine presence, more manifest at some times than others, but always there. God may be hidden and not directly manifest, but the security of the believer is analogous to the sense that a loved one is present, though in the next room. This sense of divine presence is not logically required to occur or to continue. It is a fortunate matter of fact that it happens to occur at all. To the man of secure faith it is a contingent gift.

Logical certainty is something different. Once achieved, it can be taken for granted; there is an intellectual closure to the issue. Once we have proved a theorem from a set of axioms the task is done and we go on to the next. A sense of divine presence, on the other hand, should never be taken for granted, no matter how secure the man of faith may feel, because to do so can lead to complacency and self-righteousness, obscuring the wonder that divinity discloses itself at all. Religiously the sense of presence should be felt as a mysterious gift, bestowed but not required by anything, hence, contingent. The secure believer responds with a sense of reverence and wonder. If a sense of divine presence becomes taken for granted and accepted as our just due, the religious character vanishes and self-righteousness begins to take over.

If the optimal case involving the maximum degree of a secure religious faith can rest on a contingent gift of divine presence, those of us with lesser faith should be able to accept divine contingency too.

Wavering faith and doubt may be more widespread among religious persons than is generally admitted. It may well be that, for some, it is precisely the doubt that drives them to embrace divine necessity in order to shore up the absence of secure faith.

James talks about the "once born" and the "twice born."[1] This distinction has become famous in discussions of the philosophy of religion. The once born is similar to the optimal case of the person with a secure faith. The person of secure faith is content to let things be, accompanied by a child-like acceptance of the divine gift. He asks for no further justification or proof of divine beneficence. Divine contingency should present no problem for him nor should the issue of necessity or contingency be of any concern.

Examples of the man of secure faith are easy to uncover. We can find such an example in the writer of the twenty-third Psalm. In Dostoevsky's *The Idiot* we find a sublime characterization of such a person. Others could be cited such as Brother Lawrence, the monk who can see God in the midst of cleaning the pots and pans in the monastery, many holy men, spiritual leaders and humble followers in all religious traditions. Anselm, too, may have been among these examples and out of his devotion came the ontological proof. Obviously we reject the proof, but Anselm's exercise can be seen more truly as a "testament of devotion" as I have indicated elsewhere.[2]

As for the rest of us, the twice born and those of divided mind, the possibility that there may be no divine dimension to reality at all may be only too real. For the once born, to speak of divine necessity is either pointless or an extended act of worship, a fringe benefit of reason, not required by faith. For the twice born, to speak of divine necessity may well seem absurd in the face of lingering real doubts.

Even if psychological certainty and rock-like faith were properties common to all believers, the transition to logical certainty would be questionable. There is an existential leap of faith made by many believers in "fear and trembling." Beyond this there is the complex "religious" struggle of someone like Nietzsche who is profoundly touched and bothered by the God question but is able to resolve it in the end only by an anguished and triumphant atheism. Then there are those whose faith consists mainly in hope for divine comfort and release against a background of absence and despair.

Faith and belief in God, in the absence of direct religious experience and in the presence of evil, are marvels of religious life and should command awe and respect. That it occurs at all may be a tribute to both man and God. There is real risk in religious faith, possibly more of a risk than in anything else, and the risk is that there may be no divine dimension whatsoever. The necessity of the divine existence, once accepted, bypasses the genuine gap between faith and divine absence for those who lack religious experience. Once we know that God *must* exist, the real tensions between faith and doubt would be pointless. Far from being pointless, profoundly religious lives of faith are carried out in the midst of evil and with the absence of God in experience. The marvel is that divinity seems to manifest itself in spite of all, but such manifestation can only be plausibly regarded as contingent because doubt and wonder can be present.

Philosophically, the question of God's ontological status is of interest and quite rightly so. If contingent, God is contingent in a very special sense. In the end we really don't know. I have been arguing that it seems more plausible to regard God as contingent than as necessary. Empirically, only the contingent can manifest itself, no matter how unusual and special it may be. Empirically, nature, man and God are given in terms of presentations in experience, whether directly or indirectly. What is given could just as well not be given, hence such givens are contingent.

If God is seen as a being primarily of revelation and reason, seeing Him as necessary is more plausible than if we come at the issue from the empirical side. If the experiential component is downgraded and propositional belief and dogma become the primary focus, it is easier to see God as necessary. In this case God becomes more analogous to a theoretical entity, as in science, only now God is a theoretical entity of theology.

Some would respond that theoretical entities can be perfectly real even though they are not presented in experience. Sense experience may indeed be contingent throughout, but such sense experience can point to what is a real creature of theory, a perfectly real theoretical entity, but one not manifested directly in experience. If such a situation can hold in science, why cannot religious experience point to a divinity that is not only hidden, but is also necessary?

Theoretical entities in science, though real, are creatures of theory and are also ultimately as contingent as anything else. God, the necessary being, is supposed to be ultimate outside all systems and theories. Thus, the analogy breaks down. Furthermore, divinity or God (in the context of religious worship), is not a theoretical entity (which is an abstraction) but a concrete entity who can enter into relationships with us. Divinity or God appears to be concrete, personal, existentially potent, empirical and contingent. There are theoretical components to a full fledged concept of God, to be sure, but such components are all parasitic on concrete events of divine-human encounter, which in turn are contingent. Necessity can appear in scientific theories, but ultimately all such theories are referentially directed towards the world in which we find ourselves, which is contingent. From the existential perspective, the givenness of divinity may be of over-riding importance compared to anything else. But again, importance is not equivalent to necessity.

Existentially we always confront concrete relational encounters which are contingent, whether between man and man or between man and God, where both terms of the relation are also contingent. The existential component involves the divine-human relationship as one of personal encounter, involving prayer, worship and meditation. A model of man's relation to God is the I-Thou encounter, so well described by Buber. Devotional practices in Hinduism and Buddhism diverge from this model. In these religions, relationship to a personal God does not necessarily occur, but still impingement of divinity of some sort on consciousness occurs.

God must indeed be unique as against every other kind of being. An adequate object of worship should remain unsurpassable by anything or any combination of things, including the world as a whole. Hartshorne goes on to argue that the only way to insure this uniqueness of God is that He must also be a necessary being.[3] God, indeed, would seem to be categorially unique, no matter how dimly we apprehend Him. I think it is generally agreed that God could not be just another entity in the world. It seems religiously important to see God as unique and radically different from everything else.[4]

The significant aspects of the religious life seem to have nothing to do with the logical necessity of existence. To hold that God's dependability must be grounded in His necessary existence is like saying love of one person for another can only be justified if it is provable in a strong deductive sense. Necessary truths are remote and unrelated to the existential concerns of religious faith. Faith is not a category that goes with logical necessity, for necessity carries its own warrant of rational certainty. Faith involved in the I-Thou encounter of man with God is fraught with uncertainty and anguish. Logical ground and necessary Being may also turn out to be profoundly irreligious categories. What has been arrived at through logical necessity obviates the need for faith. Suppose we were really convinced on logical grounds alone that God was a necessary ground of Being. No more ingression of the religious dimension need occur than if we were convinced that a formal proof was valid. Of course it is very doubtful that anyone was ever convinced of the existence of God on the basis of logical necessity alone. What happens is what happened to Saint Anselm; his religious faith was prior to his proof of God's necessity and so was already in place.[5]

The upshot is that nothing of any value is added to religious faith by regarding God as necessarily existent. It seems more likely that the need to establish a necessary God might evidence a lack of faith rather than support for faith. It is in this sense that ground and necessity seem to be profoundly irreligious categories.

If there is anything that seems fraught with lack of clarity or necessity it would seem to involve presentations of divinity. We try to see as best we can but in the religious domain, at best, we really do see through a glass darkly. To talk about God as a necessary being seems to obscure this religious truth. It is strange that the demand for God's necessary existence should be thought so crucial to faith. Faith reaches out in the domain of the uncertain and the unseen. We may have a deep faith in God and in divine dependability, but the faith is religiously significant precisely because of the existential uncertainty, a point Kierkegaard made quite strongly. If we get it into our heads that God necessarily exists or is the ground of Being, the need for faith would seem to evaporate. Even if we grant that a logical Ground or necessary being brings an end to inquiry, our religious encounter with the divine in experience is as far removed from this as anything could be. The God of faith is the epitome of unclear insight and mystery. Indeed, behind uncertainty there may be a discernible divine purpose. Uncertainty as to God may be required to enable us to freely respond to grace.

Religious faith has been ingrained in human culture for such a long time that, to many, divinity seems pervasive and certain. But when we consider manifestations of divinity phenomenologically, the numinous and the mysterious seem to be their most obvious features. Even the existence of things and persons in the world seems relatively obvious, but the presentation of a divine component in experience seems anything but obvious. That divinity should manifest itself at all is nothing short of sheer miracle. Such a feature is a mark of contingency though admittedly of a very special kind; miracles are anything but necessary. Again, faith, belief and wonder do not sit well with the language of necessity.

From what has been said it does not follow that rational discussion of God or natural theology is misplaced and of no religious value. Quite the contrary. We need as much reasonable explication of the concept of God as we can get, but at best all such rational approaches fall far short of making God a clearly intelligible entity. At best all our speculations and even our faith lead to scarcely penetrating the mystery of divine disclosure. We saw earlier that appeal to ultimate ground does not really provide logical intelligibility to philosophy. Even less can such an approach provide faith intelligibility to religion. That God should manifest Himself in human experience at all remains in the end a numinous mystery and a contingent act of grace and good fortune.

The important thing to keep in mind is that contingency has a strong gift-like character. What appears does not have to appear. That this is true of things in the world or of the world taken as a whole raises no objection and is obvious. That the same applies to God is questionable and is generally rejected. Yet if what we have argued is plausible, religious adequacy alone suggests that God exists contingently although uniquely, and not simply as another part of the world.

That God can appear to desert us or be absent is another reason for regarding God as a contingent being, one whose appearance, if and when it occurs, is a gift of grace. Divine absence often is due to our failure and most would argue that it is always due to our failure to believe or relate.

Apparent divine absence may be due to the fact that God does not want to control us or force us to believe. Kierkegaard presents us with the dilemma of the king who wants to court the maiden, but wants her free assent. He does not want to overwhelm her because he is a king. He wants her to accept him simply as a person. Therefore, he disguises himself so that she will not recognize him.[6]

Kierkegaard's story of the king and the maiden is very apt and may show why God remains hidden. God must not overwhelm the believer just as the king must not overwhelm the maiden. If one opted for divine necessity and accepted it fully, it is likely that the king-maiden relationship would be short circuited.

In Kierkegaard's analogy, the king must not overwhelm the maiden for a genuine I-Thou encounter to occur. Even if God existed necessarily, He would have to disguise this from the believer, for necessity would destroy the free encounter of God and man just as a royal disclosure would destroy the free encounter between the king and the maiden. Necessity seems not only redundant but destructive of the divine-human encounter.

If we can enter into a relationship with a contingent God who is only partially disclosed, why could we not enter into a relationship with a necessary being who is partially disclosed? Perhaps we could not because apprehension of divine necessity might rip the veil away and make the relationship between man and God *obligatory* rather than free. Even though God remains hidden in partial disclosure, the apprehension of Him as a necessary being might overwhelm us in the same way that the maiden would be overwhelmed if she knew the person before her was a king, even though he appeared in disguise.

When we speak of God as a necessary being there is a kind of open and shut closure that implies that we should all get in line and believe, and that it is only irrational stupidity and perversity which keeps people from accepting the divine. The exploratory existential encounter between man and God is short circuited again.

The background of objective uncertainty which Kierkegaard saw as essential to the religious life would be removed by acceptance of divine necessity. Belief in God is more appropriately accepted with "fear and trembling." I suggest that the fear and trembling reflects the real objective uncertainty that always remains in the background of religious life, even among those who are relatively secure in their faith. Agnosticism remains a live option in James's sense. Such an option would no longer make sense if God were necessary. That the ontological proof remains so unconvincing, even after being resurrected again and again, tells us something about both divine contingency and hiddenness.

If God were seen as necessary, He would stand revealed even if much remained hidden. If the being before the maiden were identified as king, he would stand revealed even though he might be elaborately disguised. The wonder and awe of religious worship require God to be a contingent gift rather than a logical truth that is to be accepted. I am reminded of a cartoon I saw some time back that showed two men looking up at the sky and pointing at a great scroll which was unrolled proclaiming, "God lives." The caption on the cartoon had one man saying to the other, "Well, I guess that settles it."

God must remain hidden so as not to overwhelm us. It would seem that once divine necessity was accepted, the lure of faith would be defeated. The king would have overwhelmed the maiden.[7]

Regarding God as necessary can lead to taking God for granted. Constant divine presence to most of us might also lead to the all too common attitude that in whatever we do God is on our side. Still, for a number of persons, the assurance that God is present does not necessarily lead to complacency.

A prime reason for regarding God as contingent is that the presence of God is even more of a mystery than the presence of things and persons in the world. It is precisely the mysterious and numinous character of religion that suggests radical contingency; thus, faith becomes the operative term in religious belief.

Ultimately it appears that divine contingency is more supportive of religious faith than rational necessity. The ultimate gift, disclosed contingently, is the gift of divinity itself. The most important gift that humans can receive is a manifestation of divinity. Such a gift is not required or deserved as a right; it is contingently presented in the most profound sense.

APPENDIX

Charles Hartshorne, more than any other contemporary thinker has pushed long and hard for divine necessity and is mainly responsible for the revived interest in the ontological proof in the twentieth century. Though many continue to disagree with him, he remains, rightly, one of the most respected and original philosophers of this century. His writings are too multiple to deal with in detail in this study, but we need to look at his view of divinity, or perfection, as he calls it, which he regards as incompatible with contingency. The heart of his objection to divine contingency is found in his book, *The Logic of Perfection*.[8]   Hartshorne maintains that there is a deficiency in failing to exist. The ordinary way of existing is a defect. The ordinary way of existing is to exist contingently. The defect is that ordinary existents just happen to exist and eventually will not. Their non-existence is a real possibility.

Hartshorne maintains that there is a basic inconsistency between perfection (God) and the possibility of not existing. He maintains that the bare possibility of not existing is a defect and hence is incompatible with perfection. As he says, "The pertinent question is not, is the fact of non-existence, but is the bare possibility of non-existence, a defect, and one which being admitted, must infect the thing *even if it exists*?"[9] Speaking of God as perfection, Hartshorne maintains that if there is even a bare possibility that God might not exist, this would be an imperfection and from this we would arrive at a contradiction in opting for a contingent God. We would be saying that perfection is imperfect. In short, according to Hartshorne the concept of a contingent God is not only false but self-contradictory as well. To exist by chance is an imperfection.

If Hartshorne is right our whole study is a pointless and self-contradictory enterprise. It is true that historically in the West God has been seen as the supremely perfect Being. Perfection, however, is an ambiguous term. To use the term the way Hartshorne does in this argument seems questionable. I suggest that religiously the term has nothing to do with the maximal modal status of necessity. The term, for the believer, designates God's overwhelming goodness and concern which makes Him alone an object worthy of worship and devotion. It does not seem that even the possible failure to exist is an imperfection in any *religiously* relevant sense.

As we shall see later, God must indeed be a unique being, but He can still be unique and remain contingent. Ordinary contingent things are radically precarious, coming into and going out of existence continuously. God is considerably less precarious, remaining existent through time.

Perfection is an abstraction but God is concrete. Hartshorne maintains that God, too, is a concrete individual and that perfection is a class of similar and genetically related states of one individual, namely God. Perfection is not a property of similar individuals; it has a unique individual referent. Again, if perfection applies only to God (and certainly there doesn't seem any reason to apply it to anything else), then if the possibility of non-existence is an imperfection, a contingent God would be a self-contradiction. The point is, it is highly questionable in terms of the religious life of prayer and worship that the possibility of non-existence is an imperfection. As we shall see, God must remain a unique and special individual, different from anything else, but that He lacks necessary existence does not detract from His religious efficacy. A being vastly superior to man in power, love and concern is a religious requirement but such superiority does not require necessary existence. Whitehead's concept of God has the requisite superiority without requiring necessary existence.

At the root of Hartshorne's view is what he calls the old insight that perfection characterizes a unique individual rather than a class of possible perfect beings.[10] Hartshorne argues that the perfect being cannot in principle be surpassed by any others but may surpass itself in a future state. It is this "cannot in principle" that makes Hartshorne require divine necessity to maintain unsurpassability in principle. Our contention is that this is not needed. All that is required of an adequate concept of divinity is that empirically it is highly unlikely that it will ever be surpassed by contingent beings other than itself.

Hartshorne does not deny that God has contingent attributes but only that God could exist contingently, that is, possibly fail to exist. Still, what Hartshorne calls the Logical-Type objection to the ontological proof seems sound. Speaking of it he says:

> Existence is on a different logical level, or of a different logical type, from a predicate, being more concrete, and hence an addition to the mere predicate, not contained in it... . A mere universal or definable abstraction such as "perfection"...cannot entail an actual individual exemplifying the universal... .[11]

Elsewhere Hartshorne makes an interesting observation which softens somewhat his radical rejection of divine contingency:

> The contingent is always something 'instead of' something else which is incompatible with it. But suppose an assertion compatible with any positive and consistent hypothesis; if such an assertion were contingent, this would be at least a very unusual type of contingency.[12]

Exactly. What we are saying is that God is contingent and that it indeed is a very unusual type of contingency. It might seem that the distinction between "very unusual type of contingency" and "necessary existence" is a trivial one and is only semantic. However, there is a world of difference between contingency, no matter how unusual, and necessity of existence. Divine necessity is incompatible with the realities of the spiritual life we live.

Hartshorne's general position is that contingency is specific, exclusive and restrictive....e.g., "x is a male" excludes "x is female." Perfection is non-specific, non-exclusive and non-restrictive, its exemplification being compatible with any state of affairs. Therefore, the concept of divinity or perfection is not contingent. Our view is that there can be, and is, a special inclusive kind of contingency, not inclusive of all conceivable possibilities but of all that are likely to occur empirically. This is sufficient for an adequate concept of God. We must ask more of an adequate concept of God than James does but far less than Hartshorne requires. If divinity had not already manifested itself empirically, the whole discussion would be pointless.

NOTES

1. William James, *The Varieties of Religious Experience* (New York: Longmans, Green and Co., 1902) Lectures IV, V and VIII.

2. See my *Intimations of Divinity*, Chapter 2.

3. Charles Hartshorne, *Man's Vision of God* (New York: Harper and Row, 1941) Chapter IX.

4. See Chapter IX.

5. In conversation with me, Raymond Anderson, a professor of Religion Studies and a colleague of mine, tells me that the Latin term for "demonstration" meant to "show forth" or "explicate," not "demonstrate" in the eighteenth and nineteenth century sense. He feels that Anselm has been misread on this point and contrary to providing a proof of God's external necessity, Anselm's position is close to mine. There is no question that faith is primary for Anselm but that his position is close to mine seems doubtful.

6. Soren Kierkegaard, *Philosopical Fragments* (Princeton, NJ: Princeton University Press, 1974) pp. 32−39.

7. In Kierkegaard's story the king actually *becomes* the peasant, just as in Jesus, God *becomes* man.

8. Charles Hartshorne, *The Logic of Perfection* (LaSalle, IL: Open Court Publishing Company, 1962).

9. *Ibid.*, p. 61.

10. *Ibid.*, p. 62.

11. *Ibid.*, p. 46.

12. *Ibid.*, p. 68.

CHAPTER VIII
THE ISSUE OF RELIGIOUS ADEQUACY

In an earlier chapter[1] we raised the issue of what would constitute an adequate object of worship. We must look into the question of religious adequacy further because it will have a major bearing on the plausibility of viewing divinity as contingent. The most serious criticism of viewpoints that regard God as contingent is that such views are religiously inadequate.

The fact that all kinds of things have been worshipped over the centuries does not indicate that such objects are adequate entities to worship. If someone feels that what he is worshipping is adequate at the moment, it does not follow that what he is worshipping will prove to be adequate in the future, particularly when the going gets rough.

Ordinary inanimate objects quickly fail us as objects of worship. Such worship restricted divinity too much to specific objects; this was divine finitude with a vengeance. Animism must be differentiated from taking objects as symbolic of divinity which is completely different. Statues of the Buddha and the Christian cross have such symbolic reference. Some Zen Buddhists argued that statues of the Buddha should be destroyed from time to time because of the danger of worshipping the statue instead of what it stood for.

Greek and Roman gods proved too anthropomorphic. They had more power than humans but ethically they were not superior to humans. They were jealous and quarrelsome; humans such as Socrates and Plato far exceeded them in ethical and spiritual awareness. Sophisticated Greeks and Romans ceased to believe in them and adopted a more abstract religious approach. While the anthropomorphism was too extreme, nevertheless, the importance of relating to a personal Thou was recognized in such religions and has remained a part of popular religion to this day.

An important aspect of religious adequacy is the transition from seeing divinity in magical terms to seeing divinity in worshipful terms. In magic, we attempt to control divinities by special incantations and rites of one kind or another. In magic we recognize the presence of supernatural powers, but we seek to control them for our own purposes.

It has been suggested to me that more sophisticated folk may attempt the same thing by developing concepts of religious adequacy. This should serve as a warning that while we legitimately seek to understand divinity more fully, our discussions of what constitutes adequacy will always fall far short of divinity itself. It well may be that God determines what is adequate for us rather than our setting up the parameters. This realization does not erase the obligation to think the issue through as best we can, but it can help us to approach the task with more humility.

Control and manipulation to enhance ourselves and destroy our enemies are the main factors in magic. When the transition to worship occurs, recognition of the autonomy of spiritual powers occurs. In worship we begin to recognize that the divine is something more than a supernatural flamethrower that we can manipulate. We recognize a spiritual force or forces with which we must deal, or come to terms; divinity can no longer be manipulated. The transition from magic to worship is not sudden or clear-cut, nor does the temptation to regard divinity magically ever disappear completely. We continue to try to manipulate divinity in various ways and in varying degrees, but what develops more strongly is the recognition of a larger center of consciousness to which we must relate on its own terms.

The issue of what constitutes an adequate object of worship is closely tied to the question of what it is to outgrow a concept of divinity. To a degree this process of outgrowing a concept of God occurs to all of us. As small children most of us can't help thinking of God as a very special person, in our society a dominant male figure, presumably like grandfather with a white beard. Even at an early age we find God to be a very peculiar "person." We never can see Him nor does He live in a house and pay rent. We learn that He is very special in peculiar ways and like nothing else whatsoever. If we remain very literal minded, tied to the concrete things of everyday life, we may tend to lose interest in God and cease to believe unless some personal crisis comes along to push us out of this stance.

Who is to say that we should outgrow a particular concept of God? The childlike naive approach, while mistaken in its literalism, is something we dare not lose altogether. Jesus said that unless we become as little children we will not enter the kingdom of heaven. Outgrowing a concept of God is not something we should do but rather it occurs naturally when we wake up one day and find that the concept of God we are attached to no longer fulfills our religious needs and concerns.

A more usual example of outgrowing an idea of God is that of some people raised as strict Biblical fundamentalists who find their childhood God to be grossly inadequate. They were raised in an environment where God is conceived more or less as a spoiled, regal potentate. This aspect makes its debut in the Hebraic tradition where Jehovah is seen as a jealous God, punishing any who seek to worship other gods. In the fundamentalist Christian tradition this Hebraic aspect of God gets grafted on to Christianity and God becomes a fearsome creature threatening hellfire and damnation to anyone who rejects or questions Him.

The doctrine of a wrathful God often gets combined with a Christian "imperialism" where accepting Jesus is seen as the only way in which revelation can be manifested and salvation achieved and where others must be converted or assigned to damnation. Needless to say, many theologians would see such Christian "imperialism" as a major distortion both of what Jesus said and of what he intended.

Many ethically and religiously sensitive persons, given this exposure to religion, reject it outright and, instead, embrace various kinds of atheism and agnosticism. It is a tragedy that many, seeing only a God of hellfire and damnation, reject religion altogether, unaware of other fruitful religious options that are available.

The concept of a God of punishment attempts to incorporate the idea of ethical duty and justice into divinity; attempting to do this by making God a dominating and jealous potentate makes a God of this nature religiously inadequate because many persons will possess qualities of character that this God would know nothing about, let alone possess.[2] It is hard to see how a loving God could also be a jealous God because many persons are loving, and not jealous, and thus would possess spiritual properties that a jealous God would lack. Within Christianity there remains a radical incoherence in attempts to combine a jealous and vengeful God with a God of love and concern. Failure to push for a more adequate doctrine of God will mean that many will conclude that religious belief is not plausible. Such persons will outgrow this God, either rejecting religion altogether or opting for a concept of God that seems more adequate.

The reader may still ask, "Who are we to determine what is adequate, accepting and rejecting concepts of God as it suits us?" The issue must indeed be approached with caution and humility. However, I think it can reasonably be said that if a person is capable of exhibiting ethical and spiritual qualities that surpass the ability found in a particular concept of God, then that concept is inadequate and falsely characterizes God.

Whitehead has made a profound attempt to develop the concept of a God of love in a more explicit direction than has been done heretofore. Rejecting the model of God as an Oriental despot, Whitehead argues that God's activity in the world is one of gentle persuasion rather than of threat or force.[3] His entire metaphysical position involves the crucial insight that God constantly participates in the creative processes of the world. The choices that we make in the world are ours and we are responsible for them but God acts as a lure, urging us to make the ethically better and more creative choice in a particular situation. Thus, God is a participant in all human choices even though an unknown one. Even when the divine lure towards the best is rejected, God is still a participant in the process but more like an advisor whose advice has been rejected. Both God and man must live with the consequences of human choice, be it good or bad.

The finite aspect of Whitehead's finite-infinite God is apparent in that God cannot force a decision; He can only persuade. It is not that God will not force a decision; God cannot force a decision. Whitehead rejects the frequent Western view of God as a domineering entity which brings his insight closer to Eastern views of divinity where the domineering aspect is less apparent or is absent altogether. In the Western theological tradition, the caretaker image of God is a more central idea than that of the domineering image. The latter image has been incorporated into the driving force behind Western technological and military expansion. The picture of divinity as acting by persuasive love rather than force is also more coherent with widespread religious experience than the domineering picture of God, thus opening up the possibility of a more religiously adequate picture of God than we have had previously.

A very common approach to divinity sees God as a device for answering prayers of a very specific nature such as prayers for good luck and good fortune and victory over our enemies. Up to a point it is obvious that this is what we would pray for but, pushed to the extreme, this approach comes close to magic again. God is seen as a kind of supernatural Santa Claus whose function is to produce what is prayed for. There have been cultures where the gods are punished if they don't produce what is requested. They are punished by having their statues put out of the temples and into the forest until they learn what a god is supposed to do. The attitude of some today is not far different from this primitive response.

While we may never give up praying for specific things altogether, many outgrow this approach by realizing that a major purpose of prayer and worship is to relate to God in a way that enhances our own sensitivity towards others in the world around us. Recognition of this factor occurs in the prayer "not my will but thine be done." The prayer sounds simple but is exceptionally difficult to will or carry out. Deciding what is God's will is one of the most perplexing and difficult problems in religion. A persistent tendency is to identify God's will with what we want to do. While God is a factor in human choice, the choice is always ours.

The most crucial issue concerning an adequate object of worship concerns finding a concept of divinity that can encompass the excruciating problem of evil, both natural and man-made, in the world. The problem is particularly troublesome given a personal theistic God who is both all-powerful and all-good. If God is all-powerful and all-good, how is it possible that He permits the obvious evils in the world?

On the issue of evil, pantheism appears to have a more adequate concept of divinity than theism. No personal God is involved. Since divinity is identified with the whole universe, no question about how God could allow evil to occur arises. What we regard as good and evil are both incorporated within divinity. In a view such as this, good and evil primarily reflect our responses to what we find in the world.

While this pantheistic view has an initial plausibility, difficulties soon manifest themselves. It is difficult to see how the whole universe can be considered divine if all the evils in the world including the holocaust are part of divinity. To accept all that occurs as equally divine blots out important moral distinctions that are essential to make. Furthermore, as we saw earlier, an adequate object of worship would seem to require some personalistic aspect in order to exceed the conscious awareness of the worshipper. Since the worshipper is a person, the "object" worshipped should be at least personalistic enough to understand and relate to the worshipper. The "object" of worship should exceed the worshipper in personalistic aspects or else we would only have one limited finite thou in relation to another finite thou.

The latter is the kind of relation that exists between persons but not the kind that relates persons to divinity. At the same time divinity is much more than a super person. Divinity is not *a* person because, while containing personhood as an aspect, it exceeds the category of personality in many ways unknown to us. Thus, the requirements of religious adequacy would seem to point towards some kind of theism.

Theism has its own difficulties, particularly if God is regarded as all-powerful and all-good. The difficulties are mitigated considerably if the concept of God includes a finite aspect and this approach has been developed in considerable detail.[4] Even given a concept of a personal God who is infinite in some respects and finite in others, difficulties remain. Richard Rubenstein, once a Jewish theologian, has rejected the traditional concept of God because he finds it morally incoherent that any such God could be embraced in the face of the enormity of evil manifested in the holocaust.[5] Attempting to combine the idea of God's chosen people with the Nazi experience defies all comprehension. What Rubenstein finds himself left with is a religious attitude towards a world without God. Whether such an approach makes sense itself is a debatable question, but Rubenstein raises the important issue which must be faced. Considering what we have confronted in the twentieth century alone, is any concept of God likely to be adequate?

Given the nature of radical evil in the world, it is hard to see how a coherent doctrine of God can be combined with the existence of such evil. I use the term "radical evil" to designate the enormity and extensiveness of unmerited suffering by millions of people. If we talk about individual suffering and pain as a source of spiritual growth and development, the dimensions of radical evil remain hidden. Even at the individual level, pain and suffering do not necessarily lead to spiritual growth. When we turn to the mass suffering from starvation and torture of millions that we have seen in this century, the dimensions of radical evil become more apparent. In terms of sheer numbers most people in the world go to bed ill-fed and ill-clothed. Given the enormity of radical evil, Richard Rubenstein finds the standard concepts of God inadequate to the situation and he is certainly not alone in this reaction.

Theodicy is the attempt to justify the ways of God in the face of evils in the world. An extensive literature already exists on this topic and to attempt a theodicy here would be presumptuous on my part as well as being beyond the scope of this work. We must say something about the issue, however, as it has bearing on the question of forming a concept of divinity that has religious adequacy.

While we can make some inroads on the problem, we are deluding ourselves if we think that a rational resolution of the problem is possible. In the end, like Job, we are forced to accept in faith, or reject without faith, the joint presence of God with radical evil. Attempts to resolve the issue by reason alone have a flavor of patent sophistry.[6]

However, some tentative suggestions and clues can be put forward in terms of the requirements of religious adequacy. Any adequate concept of God must include the idea that God suffers along with and participates emotionally with humans in the human drama. The symbolism of the cross in Christianity is a particularly dramatic illustration of this point. In orthodox terms it is said that Christ died for our sins, that God becomes man, is crucified and rises again. In other words, it is religiously essential that God enter into the life of man intimately, suffering and experiencing what man suffers, while still possessing a transcendent aspect that may pull us towards further development.

Religious adequacy does not require that we all become Christians. Religious adequacy does require that we take the symbolism of the cross seriously, that God participate with us in all our experiences, not only the bad, but the good as well. A God who only knew of our sufferings in an abstract way, as an external observer, would be religiously inferior to many persons because there are many persons who do enter into the sufferings of others in a shared way.

An adequate concept of divinity would seem to require that such divinity at least understand suffering and sympathize with it. If the symbolism of the cross is taken seriously it would seem that divinity would actually suffer along with us the events we undergo. It is the insight of various religious thinkers that God, in fact, does share emotionally in the experiences we have. Nothing can occur to us that God cannot relate to emotionally and feel along with us. Human life at its best is complex and difficult and at its worst, intolerable. Religion can be a major support for us in the sense that divinity shares experientially in our journeys.

The suffering divinity is not a central feature of pantheism as it is of Christianity. Life is just as much of a struggle, but such tranquillity as we find is due to our own meditative efforts. In naturalistic views we survive and make out the best way we can.

At this point, one might say that the adequacy requirement that God suffer along with us is nothing more than a childish Freudian wish for a super daddy to restore the lost security of childhood to us. We would like the cosmic home to feel as secure to us as was our childhood home. Aside from the fact that many had anything but a secure childhood home, this response seems too simplistic.

Existence in the world is in some ways like walking through a minefield. Even in the best of circumstances, life seems to present us with a series of tests or obstacles to overcome. The ancient myths of heroes overcoming dragons and of knights winning battles is indicative of how strongly human consciousness has read experience as precarious and threatening though often rewarding too. The lessons we learn are hard to master and, while we do learn, often it is too late. As the old Amish saying goes, "too soon old and too late smart." We are no longer in the garden of Eden; life is unfair and empirically absurd in many ways. It is also wonderful and breathtaking.

Into this cosmic drama, fraught with ambiguity, come what Peter Berger calls "signals of transcendence" and what I have called intimations of divinity. Into the life of some comes the astonishing feeling of being loved and supported by some transcendent source, different from our family and friends. Such feelings can occur with good times but surprisingly can manifest themselves in the worst of times too. This situation obviously does not occur all the time; indeed, it may not occur most of the time, but that it occurs at all is noteworthy. When such feelings do occur they are often accompanied by the feeling that there is a shared awareness of what we are going through or suffering.

That all reaching out to God should be explicable as childhood wish fantasy seems doubtful. In such situations divinity discloses another aspect to us and a religiously adequate concept of divinity must incorporate the phenomenological experiences we have described. One way of incorporating such experiences is to say that God suffers, along with us, the trials we undergo and, by such participative sufferings, supports us.

A rationalistic orthodoxy holds on to the idea that God must be infinite in all respects, all powerful and all good. To accept this, however, is to make God an accomplice in the existence of radical evil. If we accept orthodoxy, then the logic of Rubenstein's rejection becomes apparent. God would become morally responsible for evil. His moral responsibility would be due to the fact that being all-powerful, He could have removed the evil but did not. While man would obviously be blameworthy, an all-powerful God would share partial responsibility for evil by allowing it to occur in the first place. Orthodoxy has tried to avoid this conclusion in various ways but the methods attempted lack plausibility. It is hard to avoid at least partial divine responsibility for evil if God is all-powerful. A partially finite contingent God is a far more adequate object of worship. A partially finite God would undergo or experience the sufferings of the world with us; this He could not avoid, but He would not be a willing accomplice to radical evil. At the same time, the believer must have faith that divinity will not become overwhelmed by what it experiences. The believer must have faith that spiritual support continues, no matter what. This cannot be an item of knowledge, however, but must be held in faith.

We must not fall into the trap of identifying an adequate object of worship with our own religious preferences. It is easy to do this, particularly unconsciously. What constitutes an adequate object of worship may involve a contribution from various religious traditions. Through the symbolism of the cross, Christianity has given us the important insight that divinity has the ability to suffer the consequences of our actions along with us. The emphasis on human dominance over the rest of the non-human world that one finds in some kinds of Western theism is far inferior, from an environmental perspective, to some other religious traditions. Even if one regards man as a shepherd over the rest of creation, a patronizing paternalistic aspect still appears which is absent in some native American religions.

Many so-called primitive religions, particularly some of these native American religions, have a far more adequate concept of divinity that is in harmony with nature and which entails that humans must be in harmony with nature too instead of dominating it or even shepherding it on God's behalf. Hinduism and Buddhism seem more coherent on this point than does Western Christianity.

While we saw that the Western emphasis on divine personality is an important component of divinity, we need to balance the emphasis on personality with the more numinous and transcendent aspects of divinity that we find in Hinduism and Buddhism. Christianity has a danger of becoming too anthropomorphic, tending to make a super-person of God, more like the gods of Greek mythology. While God as personal must be able to relate to persons, there is much more about God that we just do not know. The numinous and transcendent factors must be kept in mind. While God may be personal, nevertheless, "His ways are not our ways."

It has been felt that a basic requirement of religious adequacy is the absolute dependability that the believer must have in the object of worship. It is generally felt that no contingent object can provide this ultimate dependability. First of all, such an object may cease to exist at any time. True, the sun and the moon do not seem likely to disintegrate any time soon but there are other features of religious inadequacy that would apply to them.

We depend on other persons, particularly those close to us, but not in an absolute sense. To require that any person be absolutely dependable or an object of worship is to require too much.

If persons prove inadequate as objects of worship, it is even more apparent that social institutions and physical objects are inappropriate objects of worship. The worship of social institutions, whether the church, the state or the party, has had devastating consequences in history which we need not re-catalog here.

A crucial factor in worship is that the object worshipped must remain superior to the worshipper in religious terms. The object worshipped may be superior to the worshipper in respects that are not crucial to the act of worship. The sun remains vastly superior to us in many ways, but it remains an inadequate object of worship because we have conscious awareness and it does not. The superiority of the object worshipped consists in its ability to absorb or relate to any act of meditation or prayer carried out by the worshipper. If the worshipper has needs which the object does not or cannot fulfill, the object is inadequate. The sun is incapable of responding to the prayers and supplications of worshippers.

In religious terms, having conscious awareness is a superior quality to lacking conscious awareness, because meditation, prayer and worship can only be carried out by conscious beings, and prayer and meditation require some response from a superior consciousness. It is true that we can rigorously meditate or center our attention upon inanimate objects. In fact, meditation practices often center on such objects. The worshippers in this situation are superior to the object on which they meditate. Doesn't this violate what we have just said? Adequate and sophisticated meditation practices often involve intense concentration on inanimate objects. On closer examination, however, it appears that concentrating our attention on inanimate objects is a device for heightening our spiritual awareness and discipline so that we can relate to the divine component of the universe, rather than making the inanimate objects themselves objects of worship. The objects become simply means towards a heightened spiritual state.

Some further questions may still puzzle us at this point. Given that we may meditate on the divine component in the universe, does it follow that such a component is necessarily conscious? Do pantheistic doctrines entail that the universe, as such, is conscious? When the individual soul achieves enlightenment by merging into a Buddhist Nirvana, does it follow that such a merger is with a conscious being? Suppose we meditate on the vastness of the universe and seek through such meditation practices to merge with the universe in some kind of spiritual union? The universe would presumably be impersonal and unconscious, and thus, inferior to the worshippers. Much Hindu and Buddhist worship is of this nature.

If an impersonal universe is worshipped by humans who possess consciousness and personality, then such worship would presumably be idolatry. The universe would be an inadequate object of worship. The theistic viewpoint maintains that the only adequate object of worship is a conscious, personal divinity, namely God. Pantheism is the doctrine that divinity is to be identified with the universe; such pantheism is a marked feature of Hinduism and Buddhism. To call Hinduism and Buddhism idolatrous seems pretentious, to say the least.

It is worth noting, however, that while philosophically Buddhism and Hinduism are pantheistic, when we turn to popular Buddhism and Hinduism, as widely practiced, personal gods and divinities abound. This may be an indication that in the active life of daily worship and meditation the object or objects worshipped need to be personal and conscious. Abstract pantheism is a doctrine which may be easier to maintain on an intellectual philosophical level than in the active life of religious meditation and worship.

On the issue of a personalistic divinity, theism may represent a more profound insight into what an adequate object of worship is than does pantheism. Buber's insight may be helpful here. An adequate object of worship involves an I-Thou encounter between the worshipper and the object (or better, subject) worshipped, where the Thou possesses the qualities of consciousness and personality. It may just be that in spite of the profound spiritual insights of pantheistic mystics, the category of personhood may give a deeper insight into the nature of divinity than can be attained by pantheism. If such be the case, we might be advised to give up the idea that separate personhood is an illusion, part of the veil of maya. Ego gratification is indeed a block to spiritual development but personhood may be a profound requirement of religious worship and growth, an I and a Thou in communion and community together.

In terms of religious adequacy, divinity must exceed any state of consciousness that humans might conceivably grow into.[7] If humans exceed the object worshipped in religiously crucial ways, then that object of worship becomes inadequate. Specifically, the believer must have faith that nothing he thinks or feels will be too much for divinity to comprehend. Divinity must be able to embrace anything that is "thrown at it." It would seem as though some kind of personalistic theism is called for in the active life of religion. To embrace and accept any personal consciousness that is thrown at it, divinity would have to be at least personal as well as obviously much more than personal.

This does not mean that the Judeo-Christian tradition, as it stands, will meet religious needs of adequacy. There are severe inadequacies in certain aspects of the Judeo-Christian concept, which further insight may rectify. As we have seen, Buddhist and Hindu pantheism do contain personalistic elements in divinity, at least as far as the average follower is concerned.

Nevertheless, for many mystics, religious adequacy seems to require only a vague impersonal divinity into which the self can merge and become obliterated. The Hindu vision of salvation uses the analogy of the raindrop that falls into the ocean. Does the raindop exist any more? Certainly not as a separate raindrop but, on the other hand, it continues to exist as part of the larger ocean. Personalistic aspects seem to be totally absent from the religious state culminating in Nirvana. In fact, in this view, it is precisely separate personhood that is the chief hindrance to salvation. To call such a view inadequate seems ludicrous since the concept of merging into a state of Nirvana represents a very sophisticated religious viewpoint. Nevertheless, it may be a real deficiency of this viewpoint that it does not give due regard to the spiritual importance of personhood for both man and God.

One might wonder why personhood is such an important category religiously. Many Oriental and some Western thinkers see personhood as the real barrier to spiritual growth and development. Such thought regards the function of religion as being precisely the elimination of our sense of separate identity and personhood.

The so-called self-contained ego which seeks only to gratify its desires, no matter how esoteric they may be, is a barrier to spiritual growth. This is a real problem because today we are conditioned more than ever before that the main function of a person is to consume and consume so that the economy can flourish. Being such consuming entities as we are, we stand a good chance of ruining the planet for all life. The lesson is not that we should cease to consume; that is absurd, but we should modify our view of personhood and see ourselves in a different light. We must reject the twentieth century view of man which increasingly can be characterized by changing Descartes's definition to "I consume, therefore I am."

One must differentiate what personhood at its best can be from what ego-gratification at its worst can be. Persons are, phenomenologically, rich centers of experiential awareness of the world around them and of other persons in the world. Persons are essentially social. We are interactive persons in community with others. In these social interactions, we do not merge or meld our consciousness with others into an organic group mind. We maintain our own distinct personal integrity and characteristics in our relationships with others whether the relationships are good or bad.

In the I-Thou encounter between one person and another, the two remain distinct, no matter how intimate the relationship. It takes two or more to be social. One cannot do it alone. The relationship between man and divinity may also be a social one at its deepest level, requiring distinct personal relationship between both, as Buber has stressed so well.

Reincarnation doctrines present interesting problems as regards personhood. If we accept such a doctrine, what is it about each person that supposedly "carries over" to the next world? We do not have the cement of more or less continuous memory that we have in this life. If memory is absent, why say that we are reincarnated? Empirically, we seem to have two different persons. If when we leave this body all our memories cease too, our personhood comes to an end just as it does in any kind of naturalistic viewpoint. On the issue of personhood, reincarnation seems to have no more religious adequacy than empirical naturalism or Western theism.

Whether we accept reincarnation doctrines or not, growing personal development seems to be of major importance in spiritual growth whether we are Christian, Hindu or Buddhist. Personhood as a property of God seems to be a crucial factor in developing an adequate concept of divinity.

We must remember that we are not dealing with views that are either completely adequate or inadequate. Rather, we are dealing with visions of divinity that involve degrees of religious adequacy. The major religions of the world have provided us with profound concepts of divinity, but each contains some inadequacies. While Western theism presents us with a personal God, the view is often too anthropomorphic, describing God as a jealous, secular ruler. We have also seen that the absolute, infinite God of classical, Western theism is a markedly inadequate concept when faced with the problem of evil. We might go on to mention the inadequacy of a purely male divinity. Such inadequacies do not invalidate a reasonably worked out idea of a personal God. In a similar way, Hindu and Buddhist pantheism may be deficient because of giving insufficient attention to personhood as part of divinity. Selfishness is one thing but personhood is something else. While selfishness can be a block to religious enlightenment, the idea of a maturing and developing person may be something to be retained rather than eliminated in the ocean of Nirvana. The lack of the personalistic emphasis does not invalidate the genuine spiritual insights of Hinduism and Buddhism, however.

What we have are partial insights into a divinity that constantly eludes our grasp. A naturalist would argue that all this talk of religious adequacy only reflects religious needs that persons have. There may be no divinity whatsoever. In that case all we are talking about is psychology. All concepts of divinity may just be projections of religious needs that get attributed to divinity. To outgrow a concept of divinity may only be to ask something different of the universe than what one asked for before. This whole chapter of our study may be simply an exercise in religious psychology, a study of what people have demanded of the universe.

We must admit that the criticism sounds reasonable. Divinity is not subject to proof or demonstration, but then neither is atheism. There are two approaches that can be taken, both quite rational and legitimate. One approach is to speak only of psychological needs. The other is to accept the psychological needs as a partial factor but then to move on to see religious adequacy as a process of genuine divine *disclosure*, where divinity manifests further aspects of itself as we become open to such disclosure. Humans may demand more of divinity than they did before, but it could also be the case that the more sophisticated demands reflect further disclosure of the divine itself. The latter approach is the one taken in this study.

In any case, an adequate object of worship is intrinsically superior to the worshipper. It has been argued that this is impossible given a contingent divinity. This is the issue to which we now must turn.

NOTES

1. See Chapter V.

2. The main Hebrew and Christian tradition sees God's justice as a *contributory* (gracious giving) justice and not *retributive*.

3. A.N. Whitehead, *Process and Reality* (New York: Harper Torchbooks, 1960) Part V, Sec. 2. and *Religion in the Making* (New York: Meridian Books, 1960).

4. William James, *The Varieties of Religious Experience* (New York: Longmans, Green and Co., 1935); Alfred North Whitehead, *Process and Reality* (New York: Harper Torchbooks, 1960); Charles Hartshorne, *Man's Vision of God* (Hamden, CT: Archon Books, 1964).

5. Richard Rubenstein, *After Auschwitz* (Indianapolis: Bobbs-Merrill, 1966).

6. See my *Intimations of Divinity*, Chapter 8.

7. Without accepting John Hick's phenomenal-noumenal approach to divinity, his approach to seeing personhood as but one aspect of the divine goes a long way towards developing a coherent view congenial to both theists and pantheists. John Hick, *An Interpretation of Religion* (New Haven: Yale University Press, 1989, Part V).

CHAPTER IX
CONTINGENT DIVINITY AND RELIGIOUS ADEQUACY

We now must deal with the question of the religious adequacy of a contingent divinity. We have seen many reasons why a contingent divinity is considered not only an implausible idea but possibly a self-contradictory one as well. Most theologians and philosophers of religion reject the idea outright.

From an empiricist perspective, necessity is manifested in the relation between statements in theories. The world as experienced contains causal connections which are contingent. The world as described by a theory may contain necessary relations, but such theoretical description is an abstraction from direct experience. The necessity resides in the connectedness between the statements in the theory. In the world as experienced contingency reigns. The world, as we experience it, is rich with connectedness and holistic in nature. Experience is more accurately described by James and by Whitehead than it is by Hume. Even in the modern "rich" view of experience, it does not follow that the connectedness we experience involves logically necessary relations. In the discussion to follow we will be talking about our experiences rather than about the world directly.

As far as our experiences of divinity are concerned, they are numinous and religiously suggestive of a rich divine reality. The interpretations and religious beliefs that stem from such experiences are another matter. Nowhere in such experiences is there a place for logical necessity.[1] Necessity can only be imported into our religious experience by explicit appeal to reason and revelation as found in theological system building.

Earlier we talked a great deal about gifts. Of all gifts that we receive, the gift of divine grace, when it occurs, seems the most significant and far-reaching. No gift is of more importance. No gift is more unexpected than this. The gift-character of divinity is particularly apparent if love and concern are crucial aspects of God.

Love and concern, whether manifested by one person to another or by God to man, are manifestations that do not have to occur, that possess no necessity about them whatsoever. The gift character of love and concern manifests contingency if anything does. Love and concern, being such crucial parts of divinity, suggest divine contingency.

That any entity, whether human or divine, can manifest love, compassion and concern seems remarkable and clearly devoid of necessity. It may be said that only God's existence is necessary, not the gifts that He chooses to bestow upon us. Nevertheless, love, concern and compassion seem to belong to what traditionally was called the essential nature of God. Without embracing essentialism we might note that as divine disclosures accumulate, the qualities of love, concern and compassion seem increasingly important and significant. These qualities seem to be a part of what Whitehead calls God's primordial nature.

One might still insist that necessity applies only to the divine existence and that everything else that can be said about God is a contingent manifestation of Him. Why hold on to divine necessity any longer? What gain is there? The demand for such necessity seems to reflect only a lingering rationalist presupposition of a completed and fully intelligible universe. Historically, Christianity became tied into the fortunes of Western philosophical rationalism, just as in the Middle Ages it was tied into the fortunes of an Aristotelian philosophy of nature and metaphysics. There is no good reason why Christianity in particular or religious faith in general should depend on the fortunes of Aristotle, rationalism, Whitehead or any other school of thought. Schools of thought may lend and have lent insight into divine disclosure, but such disclosure is primitive and basic in human experience. Schools of thought are helpful but in the end are finite human creations used in explanation. They come and they go, but divine disclosure continues throughout. Religion cripples itself if it ties itself too closely to any philosophical school of thought.

Experience, as well as the new findings of science, suggest an incomplete and open ended universe as James saw clearly. Complete intelligibility is not to be found. It may be used as a regulative device or norm in science and philosophy but not thought of as constitutive of things as they are.

The working life of faith has no need of divine necessity. James's "sentiment of rationality" as a regulative norm coupled with the assurance of divine reality is all that is needed in the life of faith. To opt for necessity is to make an illicit move from religious psychology to logic. Husserl attacked psychologism for confusing how the mind empirically does act with the logical question of how it should act. Reversing the terms, we might criticize theological *logicism* for confusing divine necessity with the psychological needs of the religious worshipper.

If anything could be considered the paradigm of a gift, it is love. Not only is it not required by logical necessity, it cannot even be produced on demand empirically or ethically. While it may be an ethical requirement that I treat you with respect, regardless of how I feel about you, you cannot make it an ethical requirement that I feel the emotion of love towards you. You can insist that another person respect you but you cannot insist that they must love you as a right to which you are entitled.[2]

On the basis of our vague intimations of divinity and the fact that we constantly outgrow various concepts of divinity, replacing them by others, it would seem that the divine is open ended in the sense that divinity seems capable of surpassing all our concepts. People outgrow various concepts of divinity, but humans seem incapable of outgrowing divinity itself. What is the difference between outgrowing a concept of divinity and just changing one concept of divinity for another? The idea of outgrowing a concept implies that the replacement is superior in some sense to the concept it replaced.

The changing of such concepts may say nothing about God but only something about us. This naturalistic interpretation is certainly a legitimate one to make and commits one to far less than does assuming that there is a divinity. Nevertheless, it is also possible that such changes are brought about by a further divine disclosure to the worshipper, who may now be ready for such disclosure. It is possible that worshippers may be able only to receive the disclosures of divinity that they are ready for and must work out the consequences of a given disclosure until it proves indadequate for them. We may start out only able to conceive of God as a vengeful being wielding power and coercion. After many trials and tribulations we may come to see God as loving and forgiving and as a being transcending national boundaries. We can interpret these trials as changes in human outlooks on God but we may also interpret them as involving a continuing revelation of God, requiring richer concepts of divinity than we had before. Thus, as concepts of God change, divinity itself continues to surpass all our concepts.

Marx and Freud assumed that religion was either an opiate of the people which would wither away after the revolution or else it was a childhood wish fulfillment for security that we would do away with once we grew up. Looking at the present day Soviet Union and Eastern Europe, religion is far from withering away. In the communist world religion continues to be a vital force. While religion as an influence on Western culture has waned markedly, the interest and concern with religious questions has not died out. Though God may be hidden, emptiness and alienation spur the search for human transcendence and meaning.

On the day that humans surpass their religious objects of worship altogether, when nothing further calls on us to surpass ourselves in radical ways, religious worship will be obsolete. On the day that there is no mystery or numinous character of the world to experience, religious worship will cease. On the day that we achieve complete intelligibility in our human knowledge, no worship will continue. Such a day, however, becomes more and more remote with the passage of time. Even within the domain of science itself, the more we investigate the stranger and more mysterious the world becomes. I am not denying the importance and significance of the knowledge we have and will continue to get, but we must note that the growth in human knowledge is not like closing the gap between here and a place we are going to visit as we travel towards it. The more knowledge we get does not bring us closer to some absolute cognitive goal where all is known and intelligible. No matter how much progress we attain in our cognitive enterprises, ultimate mystery remains.

The things that exceed our grasp, including the divine component in experience, exceed us to such a degree that even if divinity is contingent, it is unlikely that we could ever outgrow or surpass it completely. Divine necessity does not seem required. To insist on such necessity does little more than add a name to a mystery. In Oriental pantheism and in the religious practices of various native Americans, a sense of the all encompassing nature of the divine is all that seems required for the religious life. It is doubtful that necessity is essential in Western theistic religions either. William James, speaking to the point of what is required of divinity, remarks that, "All that the facts require is that the power should be both other and larger than our conscious selves. Anything larger will do, if only it be large enough to trust for the next step."[3]

James is correct in opting for finitude in God. To demand divine necessity is far in excess of what is needed for religious adequacy. He is wrong, however, in arguing that anything larger will do. James's doctrine of a *purely* finite God would make divinity just another part of the contingent empirical world. As we shall see later, God has to be something special and not just another item in the inventory of things in the world. Religious faith may be existentially risky, but it would become ludicrously precarious if one regarded God as only another contingent being. A form of Manichaeism would ensue where the odds would be fifty-fifty or more that God would be destroyed by the non-divine components of the world.

More significantly, *empirically*, disclosures of the divine do not function at all like the disclosures of ordinary contingent objects. Divine disclosure is often marked by strongly numinous qualities, by no simple location in a specific place and it frequently is manifested as what Otto calls the "mysterium tremendum." Furthermore, religious yearning is manifested with ubiquity in all cultures at all times.

John Smith has said that experience of God is also experience of something else at the same time. When divinity is disclosed, we "see" divinity through apprehension of ordinary contingent objects and events. Moses "saw" God in the burning bush. In the religious consciousness of many native Americans, divinity is apprehended by means of the aesthetically sublime in nature. For Protestants, God may be disclosed in the life of Christ and for Catholics, God manifests himself in the mass and in the taking of the sacraments. In all kinds of human situations involving struggle, growth and moral sensitivity, divinity may be seen to disclose itself. In all religious traditions, the lives of certain people manifest what is taken to be a divine disclosure. The Buddha and Christ are only two extremes of many examples that might be cited, taken from all cultures. Last but not least, certain historical events are taken to be of peculiar religious significance where divinity is disclosed. In the deliverance of the Jews from Egypt, the disclosure of God was apparent.

Such disclosures are epistemically tricky. In each of the examples cited above and in countless others, no divine disclosure may be apprehended at all. The burning bush of Moses can be seen as a piece of shrubbery on fire.

The taking of the sacraments can be seen as a quaint Catholic ritual with only sociological significance. The deliverance of the Jews from Egypt can be seen as but another example of gaining political freedom from oppression.

If disclosure of divinity also involves experience of some ordinary contingent event or object, the event or object in question can also be seen without any reference to divine disclosure. For Christians, Jesus is disclosed as God the Son. For non-Christians, Jesus is another in a long line of unusual spiritual leaders or possibly just another human being with some special spiritual qualities. Epistemically there is no way to prove or empirically show that divinity is also disclosed in the event or thing experienced. If divinity is disclosed it is a very special and unique kind of contingent disclosure, unlike any other, which may be what was originally intended by the special word, "revelation."

Let us assume, as we have assumed all along, that there really is such a phenomenon as divine disclosure. If such be the case, the disclosures always occur through a medium of ordinary contingent happenings. Divinity does not seem to be disclosed by itself alone. Another way of saying this is to say that God is a hidden God. God's appearance occurs within the context of ordinary contingent objects and events in which the divine factor can be interpreted out, if we so desire.

Disclosure and hiddenness occur with all disclosures of divinity. The closest analogy we have to this is the disclosure of one person to another. No matter how intimate our relations to another human being may be, there are always parts of the person that remain hidden. Indeed, even in self-consciousness there are parts of us that remain hidden from our own scrutiny. While a person is only partially disclosed to another, he can still be basically present in his totality because he is embodied unambiguously. It is at this point that the analogy with divine disclosure breaks down. We are embodied and possess simple location unambigiously in space and time. We may be at different places at different times but we can only be in one place at a time.

Whatever divine disclosure may be, it is not bound by the restrictions of embodiment and simple location.

The lack of specific unambiguous embodiment by divinity allows for a broad range of interpretation and ambiguity. No matter how complex and hidden Mr. X may be as a person, he is unambiguously an embodied person. He can, theoretically at least, be pointed to as "that person over there." Not so with divinity.

This freedom from simple location and embodiment makes divine disclosure radically different from ordinary contingent disclosure. Another feature of divine disclosure that differentiates it from ordinary contingent appearance is that the presence of God calls for a radical change of character on the part of the person having this experience. We speak of such changes of character in terms of conversion experiences or radical changes in lifestyle that occur at least temporarily when God manifests himself. Confrontation with ordinary contingent objects and events generally does not call for radical change of character, though sometimes it does.

The presence of physical objects while constantly requiring us to adjust to their presence does not usually call on us to radically change our characters for the better in moral and spiritual matters. Taking drugs in order to get a "high" may make us feel good, but generally does nothing to improve our characters or develop our personalities in significant ways. Sometimes the presence of physical objects may cause a change of character for the better. Confronted by persons "shooting up" drugs, we may be overwhelmed by compassion and decide to devote our lives to drug rehabilitation. When this latter situation does occur it may not be too farfetched to say that divinity has also disclosed itself in the situation even though the person involved might not describe it this way.

Contact with another person may also cause us to make a radical change in character and indeed those we are most intimate with do change our characters, but this may be for better or worse. The impact of Dr. Martin

Luther King caused many to devote their lives to racial harmony and justice. Such an impact of one person on others may be the closest analogy we have to the impact that God makes on us to change our lives. Many would say that it was the disclosure of God, acting through Dr. King that brought about such spiritual changes as occurred. But even personal encounter does not usually lead to radical change of character. We meet all kinds of people all the time whose impact on our basic values and concerns is negligible. For that matter, many persons met Dr. King in casual contexts of one kind or another leading to no adjustments in character as a result.

Divine disclosure does seem to be unique and does generally lead to alteration of character in a more spiritual and ethical direction. Even if disclosure of God is also disclosure of something else, character changes for the better at least seem called for. This alone makes divine contingency different from our experience of other contingent events and objects. Indeed, the very commitment to faith in God may induce a new perspective on all of one's life, though this does not necessarily happen. Many who claim a sincere faith in God remain much as they were before such a conversion. This again indicates that faith may be more like falling in love; something happens to you rather than your bringing such a state about by your efforts alone.

For some persons the entire range of their experience may become *saturated* by divinity. St. Francis comes to mind as such a person and we could find others. Though not a usual state of consciousness or even of religious consciousness, a person so saturated stands out among us as peculiarly saintly or special. To such a person, the entire contingent world appears like a precious gift. Divine saturation may occur to some only rarely and for short periods of time or possibly it may form a more or less continuous background in a person's experience. For such persons no particular contingent object or event stands out as a special vehicle for divine disclosure because all experience bears the stamp of divinity.

For most persons, however, only a small range of experience has the mark of divinity upon it. Only special objects, persons and events disclose the divine. There are also persons who feel what could be called divine "leadings" to pursue certain vocations and activities. Persons are not supposed to enter the priesthood unless they feel "led" to do so. Many others feel that their vocational and career choices are a result of divine leading. Whether this is really so or not is difficult or impossible to determine in particular cases. Nevertheless, the phenomena is so widespread that genuine divine leading cannot be ruled out a priori. In such cases God may disclose Himself but here too a contingent empirical insight is disclosed as well, namely a direction for our lives.

All examples of divine disclosure are contingent and are manifested through the objects and events which signify such disclosure. The divine component is peculiar and special and presumably the same divine component is manifested in all the instances.

It would seem reasonable to regard the divine component as being just as contingent as the things and events in which it is manifested even though contingent divinity has special and peculiar features. Introducing necessity will not help clarify matters at this point. God is indeed separable and different from ordinary contingent things. There is much more to divinity than its manifestation in any set of things or events in the world. Divinity is also separable by means of conceptual elucidation in philosophy and theology.

When we say divinity can be "seen" in the statue of the Buddha or "seen" in the distant mountains, we are dealing with a very special use of the term "seen." If experience of divinity is also experience of something else at the same time, we see two things instead of one but see each in a different sense. Anyone with functioning eyesight can see the statue of the Buddha or the distant mountains and see them without any implication that divinity is also manifested in their vision. For those who also *see* divinity, the statue and the mountains act like a transparent transmission belt for a deeper apprehension. They see or feel divinity through the statue and the mountains, but a divinity partially disclosed though still hidden. All meditation practices and worship services involve use of ordinary contingent objects and events. The same dual apprehension occurs when a devout Catholic sees the newly sacrificed blood and flesh of our Lord offered to God in the transubstantiation of the host. To the non-Catholic, atheist or literal-minded Protestant, all that is seen is a transmission of bread and wine to the believer even though the communion may be a deeply significant symbolic ritual.

Can divinity ever manifest itself without the transmission belt of contingent events? There are many reported cases where people hear direct messages from God and for devout Christians who have dreams or images of Jesus, God would seem to appear directly, unhidden. In all such reported cases some physical transmission mechanism seems involved in terms of sight or hearing. How about the still small voice of God that may speak out of the silence in a Quaker meeting? How about the voice of individual conscience?

In all such cases there seems to be a direct encounter of God and the believer without the intervening medium. Nevertheless, it is probable that some medium of transmission is present in these cases. The believer is an embodied entity and the purported direct encounters always occur in some contingent event context, be it the Quaker meeting or the searchings of conscience by someone in prison or in some other contingent situation.

There clearly is a continuum of situations here starting from ones in which God seems to manifest Himself directly, where He is felt to be closer than hands and feet to religious experiences where contingent objects and events symbolize divinity only in a remote and vague way. In all cases of divine disclosure it must be remembered that much more is hidden than is ever disclosed. Recall Kierkegaard's story of the king and the maiden.

In general I think we can safely say that divinity and contingent events in which divinity is manifested appear together in experience, though a separation can be made in acts of worship and meditation. A particularly dramatic separation is made when the Zen monk burns the statue of the

Buddha. In fact he feels it necessary to do so because often the ordinary contingent object or event "absorbs" the divine component to the extent that the worshipper engages in an act of idolatry; he worships the instrument of divine transmission rather than the divinity that is to be transmitted. This is by no means a trivial danger. Think how often churches, religious institutions and practices have become idolatrous objects of worship in themselves. The whole thrust of Protestantism is the Western equivalent of the burning of the statue of the Buddha. That Protestantism must occur again and again is testimony to the danger of taking the contingent object or event to be the divine itself. I am using "protestant" here in its root meaning of protesting against an already established tradition that seems to have gone sour.

Contingent objects and events can be and are essential as "signals of transcendence," to use Peter Berger's colorful designation. Both the signal and what it signifies are contingent though in radically different ways because both are given in experience, no matter how indirectly.

As we have already seen, divine disclosure is a very special kind of contingent disclosure, different from other kinds of contingent manifestation. Nevertheless, James is right in his basic attempt to work out a plausible doctrine of divine contingency, even though his purely finite God falls short of what is required. Given the special nature of divinity, the danger that a contingent divinity will be surpassed by something else is probably not a significant danger. The eternal aspects of God assure this.

Philosophically considered, a form of dipolar theism with a contingent God can provide a religiously adequate concept. In the view of dipolar theism, given a contingent God, all that is required is that certain divine properties be eternally manifest, stable and continuing in different divine disclosures. A certain set of stable, unchanging, divine properties is large enough to do. With these stable properties, God exhibits all kinds of contingent and changing properties as well to meet different situations.

One might ask how we know that the stable and eternal properties of

God will last if God is contingent. We don't know for sure, of course; this is precisely the point where faith enters. If we resort to divine necessity to try to cloak the gap between knowledge and faith we will add not an iota to our information.

What seems required is some sense of the eternal in our concept of divinity, but eternity is different from necessity. I would suggest, following Whitehead's lead, that God may contain certain invariant features which do not change over time. For Whitehead these features are found in God's primordial nature, which he contrasts with the changing features of God found in the divine consequent nature. The divine eternity would be manifested in the primordial nature. In specific terms God would eternally manifest love and concern for creatures, though how such love and concern is manifested would vary from one situation to another.

In terms of religious adequacy all that we could reasonably expect is that divinity encompass and exceed any human needs and expectations that might arise. Such expectation does not mean that the divine presence will be manifested at all times. Divinity is often hidden and there are times in world history and in the lives of individuals where "The gods withdraw." For many persons ours is such a time of withdrawal. The parables of Jesus concerning the absent master need to be kept in mind. Divinity may absent itself but, for the religious worshipper, such absence does not mean that divinity ceases to be or that it ceases to possess certain eternal attributes. What is required of the believer is faith that elusive divinity can manifest itself to humans at times and in ways of its own choosing.

In light of the elusive and hidden aspects of divinity, it requires a great deal of faith to believe in the eternal goodness and care given to us by the divine dimension of the world. To speak of divine necessity is to obscure the real risks involved in divine-human encounters. The whole context of faith and worship seems alien to the category of necessity.

Up to this point, we have maintained in general terms that contingent divinity is not only adequate but may even be essential for the religious life. Let us return to the specific objections to a contingent God that we surveyed earlier[4] and see how they might be answered.

Many theologians would insist that a contingent divinity is too precarious to be an adequate object of worship. Many thinkers will grant the real, existential risks for humans in acts of religious faith in the absence of solid knowledge, but they will argue that such existential risks cannot be conflated into *ontological* risks concerning the nature and status of God. The argument might be made that precisely because of the existential risks of faith commitment, such commitment must be to a being that is ontologically secure, that is to say, necessary.

I would suggest that the existential and the ontological cannot be separated in this way. Given the nature of the world we live in including the natural and man-made evils we find, real doubt as to there being any divine component whatsoever is quite reasonable. It would require a great deal of self-assurance to argue that ultimately atheism, agnosticism and naturalism arise from failure to realize that God exists necessarily. Recall at this point Richard Rubenstein's anguished search for an adequate religious expression without God.[5] Faith in divine goodness *is precarious*, both ontologically and existentially. An open and clear-eyed faith must constantly recognize that it could be completely unjustified. Dominant faith without recessive doubt ignores the terrible features that bedevil our world and tends to become dogmatic. Faith there can be, but, as Kierkegaard expressed it, genuine faith must be held with "fear and trembling." Faith is a risk towards which we are driven, more often than not, by what Jaspers called the boundary situations of life. Risk involves contingency.

Again the complaint is raised that a contingent God could fail us. How can we have faith in something that might not be? We can only say any kind of divinity we believe in might fail us. Calling God necessary does not change things one iota. Faith failure can result from the dimensions of evil and suffering in the world which, prima facie, count against there being any divine dimension at all. The reality of religious experience coupled with our ignorance of the extent of evil are two factors that help sustain faith in the face of negative experiences. Fortunate indeed are those who have a secure faith and sense of divine presence in spite of everything. For many others, faith is an existential discovery of hope out of a state of anguished despair. The fear that a purely contingent God will be surpassed by us pales against the real possibility that there may be no God at all.

The issue of whether God is necessary or contingent may in the end be an interesting logical question that theologians and philosophers concern themselves with, but the issue may appear to have no relevance at all in the active life of faith. Those who believe in God's necessary existence will respond by saying that even though the active life of faith does not require explicit concern with the issue, the only way that religious faith can be grounded and made plausible is if God is seen as a necessary being. It would be the job of the theologian to point this out, even if the believer does not have to concern herself with the issue.

Nevertheless, the doubt and existential anguish of many sincerely religious souls have ontological implications too. Given the right set of circumstances, Nietzsche's anguished cry, "God is dead and we have killed him," might be uttered by any one of us. But in this anguish there may also appear the amazing gift of grace that there is a God and that He loves us. Such a manifestation would be contingent and the manifestation of love would be radically contingent whether given to man by man or to man by God. If outreaching love were necessarily manifested by divinity, it would not be love in any sense that we could understand or relate to. A love that *must* occur is no love at all.

For those lucky enough to have the assurance of divine presence, such assurance is felt with one's whole being but has nothing to do with maintaining God's necessary existence. Anselmians have equated the two but they are mistaken, for the assurance of religious faith is deeply psychological while necessity is a purely logical category.

The problem of the absent God is one that has not received sufficient attention. God may be perfectly real but is not always present in human experience. Parables in the New Testament speak of the absent master who will return eventually and of what the servant must do during the absence of the master. The dark night of the soul, spoken of by many mystics, also gives moving reference to divine absence.

Combining divine absence with the huge dimensions of the problem of evil presents a tremendous challenge to the life of faith. Religious faith can be and is maintained in the face of these conditions, but religious faith must be aware of and sensitive to the real difficulties presented by both divine absence and the presence of evil.

Divine absence and the presence of evil seem to be further marks of divine contingency. It is true that the man of faith may continue to have psychological certainty that God's manifestation in human experience and history will continue, no matter how difficult this is to believe. But hope and faith would not seem appropriate or needed if divine necessity were opted for or divine absence never occurred. Once we know that God exists necessarily, then we should be able to sit back and relax; the tension of faith is not called for. Faith is appropriate precisely because there is no necessity. It is likely that, for a majority of believers, real evidence of divine presence is rare or else never occurs at all. For many, faith consists in belief and hope that divinity is disclosed. For a sizable minority, however, such faith is combined with a more or less continuing assurance of the presence of God in their experience, either in the form of a constant sense of divine presence or else intermittent experiences of divinity.

Resignation to an abstract divine necessity seems a highly questionable way to make up for divine absence and the need for faith. With necessity everything is clear and distinct. No loose ends remain. In the religious life of faith, we, at best, see through a glass darkly. Believing that God is absolutely dependable, no matter what the appearances, is more analogous to the limited dependability we rely on in other persons around us than to a logical doctrine of divine necessity. Believing that God is dependable, no matter what, involves reaching out to another Thou with the risk that no response will be forthcoming. Admittedly, depending on God is different in crucial ways from depending on other persons. To demand that other persons be absolutely dependable, no matter what, is to ask too much of other persons. Nevertheless, if depending on other persons is risky, dependence on God is risky too, because in both cases one must reach out towards the other in faith and hope, in advance of hard evidence that such dependence is justified. Even if one has felt support and comfort in the past, regarding persons or God as dependable involves faith and hope that such reliance will be justified in the future. Clearly, in the matter of depending, be it human or divine, the marks of contingency are manifest.

But how can one guarantee that a purely contingent divinity will remain intrinsically superior to the worshipper? It is always logically possible that any contingent entity might be surpassed. Thus, only a necessary being could remain intrinsically superior to all else and, thus, be an adequate object of worship. One can only respond by saying that in the religious life of prayer, worship and meditation, there are no logical guarantees.

Religious faith is not equivalent to absolute warranty that there is a God or that He will remain unsurpassable. This type of demand seems to be a residue of the Greek and Platonic preference for mathematical certainty. But a bothersome question may still persist. What if a contingent God should die or cease to exist? What if the failure of religious faith and worship is not due to our lack of faith, but rather to God's demise? Or, just as bad, what if God turns against me? The only appropriate response is the one made by Job, "Though He slay me, yet will I trust Him." Kierkegaard is right. Faith can only occur in the face of objective uncertainty, try to disguise it as we will. And objective uncertainty indicates contingency.

The act of faith operates in a context of uncertainty. Many would argue that the act of faith affirmation is a radical one, always attended with psychological uncertainty. When the term "certainty" is used with anything but metaphorical force, religious faith departs, and theologians are generally aware of this. Ideas of theological necessity generally concern the *inner* coherence between aspects of what is believed on faith, rather than referring to coercive logical necessity. It seems likely that a well thought out doctrine of contingent divinity could provide sufficient support to be religiously adequate. Professor George Allan, in correspondence, has made the fruitful suggestion of a special *moral* necessity in God, in which certain ethical aspects of God would be steadfast and persistent over time but God Himself would remain ontologically contingent.

The attempt to introduce divine necessity to bolster religious faith involves a "category mistake." Empirically, all that we can say is that in the religious life of prayer and worship, we find divinity to be superior, though this finding is contingent. We find empirically that divinity encompasses and surpasses all attempts to surpass it. We outgrow many concepts of God or divinity, but the divine itself always has continued to exceed our grasp. Whether this superiority will continue to be the case in the future, only time will tell. We cannot guarantee in advance that such will be the case. On the basis of past experience it seems highly likely that divine superiority will continue to manifest itself, and this, combined with faith, seems to be all that religious adequacy requires.

NOTES

1. I may state propositions about the world which are logically necessary. For example, "Every effect has a cause," but any actual causal relation, as it is experienced, is contingent.

2. I tend towards a Kantian interpretation of the religious injunction to love all mankind. As a command to produce the emotion of love, it seems patently absurd. But as a requirement of justice to respect the rights of all, regardless of feelings, it makes sense. See my *Intimations of Divinity*, Chapter 9.

3. William James, *The Varieties of Religious Experience* (New York: Longmans, Green and Co., 1935) p. 525.

4. See Chapter V.

5. Richard Rubenstein, *After Auschwitz* (Indianapolis, IN: Bobbs-Merrill, 1966).

CHAPTER X
DIVINE UNIQUENESS

The more general concept, "divinity," or the more specific concept, "God," indicates a peculiarly unique factor in the universe which is radically different from anything else. Although this study rejects God's necessary existence, we must give some kind of account of divine uniqueness which makes God's contingent existence different from ordinary contingency.

From an empiricist perspective something very strange and wonderful is occurring when divine impingement on the universe takes place. Divine impingement is strange because such impingement transcends the naturalistic world of sensory experience which is with us all the time. Most of the time we do not notice the strangeness and oddity of divine impingement because it is not an obvious and widespread feature of everyday experience and also because religious institutions have made the idea of divinity or God familiar to us whether we have religious experience or not. Otto comes closest to capturing this strange aspect of divine impingement by his discussion of the numinous and transcendent aspect of divinity in his classic work.[1]

As we have seen, viewed empirically and with a minimum of interpretation, divinity is manifested through a vague amorphous class of experiences, some dramatic, some not, which impinge on human consciousness in a variety of ways.

The vague, amorphous religious experiences do not lend themselves easily to any kind of designated uniqueness. In the theistic tradition we have stipulated divine uniqueness by use of the term, "God." By such stipulation we have designated a unique referent. It does not follow that we create or bring God into existence by such stipulation. Supplemented by reliance on revelation, theism makes a precise designation by referring to the amorphous impingements of divinity as disclosures of God. A significant reason for making a precise designation is that divine manifestation includes personalistic aspects which prove crucially significant for religious worship. In prayer and in much meditation a personal I-Thou encounter is central to the act of worship. Given the phenomenological data that shows much worship is transacted on an I-Thou basis, the amorphous impingements of divinity become focused on a unique, personalistic, specific being — God.

Whether we speak of divinity in terms of the amorphous mass of its empirical manifestations or whether we speak more narrowly of God, there are special features involved which set all such disclosures apart from ordinary kinds of unique disclosure. The empirical uniqueness of each thing and each person in everyday life is apparent to all. What divine uniqueness might be is not clearly apparent. First of all, every "thing" we encounter in the world is a member of a species or kind in the sense that there are other things like it. Every particular thing is also unique.

What gives uniqueness to every particular thing in the world is that it is embodied in space and time. Each has definite spatial boundaries and each exists for a particular time but does not exist at all times. Spatio-temporal position is the simplest way to determine the uniqueness of objects in the world though probably no two objects in the world have all other properties in common. What we have just said applies to persons too because the simplest way to identify them is by seeing their bodies. Even though we may not tend to think of persons we know in these terms, no matter how mental, spiritual and loving they may be, they, too, are embodied in space and time.

Obvious though this may be I stress the point because the

embarrassment in our dealing with divinity or God is that no uniquely designated disclosure by embodiment seems possible. Leaving aside the Christian view of Jesus for the moment, there is no unique thing that we can designate as divinity or God. Theology would be much simpler if such designation were possible.

All we can do is make some kind of designation by analogy. We say, for example, that God can be disclosed in such things as holy places, saintly persons and historical events; indeed, God's disclosure can occur anywhere at any time, but such disclosure is ambiguous and subject to multiple interpretation. To speak of God's specific embodiment seems peculiar and misleading because the only specific embodiment we know is the kind we find in the things that surround us. The latter kind of embodiment is obvious to all, the former is not, and such designation raises considerable questions.

From a monotheistic perspective, the same God discloses himself over and over again in places, persons and events. Just when and how such disclosure occurs is a matter of considerable puzzlement and debate. A major factor is that the theist sees places, persons and events as disclosing the presence or action of God.

Divine uniqueness in the form of God is most apparent in monotheistic religions. In various forms of polytheism, one unique designation is not possible at all. In pantheism, divine uniqueness is vacuous, at best. If divinity is co-extensive and identical with the whole universe or is not separable from the universe, then there is indeed a kind of uniqueness, but this says little more than that there is a universe. The significance of divine uniqueness is most apparent with doctrines of God, either theistic or panentheistic.

Viewed from a strict empiricist perspective, that the same God is manifested in different places, persons and events cannot immediately be taken for granted. There are vast differences in the manifestations involved. Nevertheless, a combination of reason and faith can bring about the required unity of diverse manifestations. After all, in everyday life and science, we bring empirically diverse phenomena together in unifying concepts, so why shouldn't the same procedure be legitimate in reference to God?

Seeing diverse phenomena as manifesting aspects of one God, rather than seeing such phenomena in polytheistic terms, may not only simplify our handling of a multiplicity of data, but may also reflect a genuine continuing divine disclosure to us as well.

If divinity could manifest a specific and unambiguous embodiment, specifying divine uniqueness would appear to be a much simpler task. However, when divinity was specifically embodied in animals, plants and other things, religious inadequacy became apparent. Specific embodiment involves radical finitude and death. If divinity were specifically embodied unambiguously in a thing, when the thing perished, divinity would perish too. Divinity, too, would just be another ordinary item of the world.

When we say that divinity or God can be manifested in holy places, saintly persons and historical events, we are talking about something quite different from specific embodiment which is what we ordinarily think of as embodiment. The empirical situations in which the divine may be disclosed are multifaceted and ambiguous. Where such disclosure occurs, divinity is not completely captured or specifically designated. Divinity remains transcendent of all disclosures.

There is a sense in which any empirical object transcends all presentations of it that occur in experience. For any given empirical object there are aspects of it that are never seen by anybody. No matter how exhaustive our analysis, we can never completely capture the concreteness of any given object by our concepts. But unobserved aspects of an empirical object could, at least in principle, be subject to some kind of observation, no matter how indirect. Even if we cannot capture a unique object completely by our concepts, the full embodiment is manifested to us concretely in experience. Divinity, on the other hand, is so ambiguous in its disclosures and so numinous and mysterious in its manifestations that a radical kind of transcendence is involved and no unique embodiment is attainable.

It is this transcendence of all disclosure and specific embodiment that gives contingent divinity the peculiar uniqueness that sets it apart from the other contingent objects of the world. That is why, in the end, we must *stipulate* divine uniqueness by designating the referent as God. While we stipulate divine uniqueness as God, there is empirical warrant for doing so, based on the disclosures of the divine that we encounter. This multiple disclosure in different times and places gives divinity its peculiar status, namely a contingent entity that can manifest itself anytime, anyplace.

If we say no more than this, divinity would be no different from the color green or any other universal, which also is contingent but with eternal manifestations. One immediate difference between divinity and the color green is that green is not manifested at all times, nor is any other universal likely to have exemplification at all times. Of more significance is the realization that while green is disclosed in multiple instances, the color green itself is an abstraction. Green can have concrete instances, sure enough, but considered as a universal, it is an abstraction. Universals are abstractions with concrete instances. Divinity, on the other hand, is concrete, manifesting itself partially in multiple disclosures which are also concrete.

We *see* God or divinity manifested in multiple situations. Such "seeing" is very tricky but phenomenologically the idea makes sense. Pantheism sees divinity manifested in everything. This produces some deep and sublime religious responses but, philosophically, to see divinity in everything, all the time, may appear to make divinity vacuous. For religious pantheists, this philosophical vacuity does not seem to matter.

Empirically, the terms, "God" or "divinity," take on more importance when we *see* the divine manifested in some things and events and not in others. For instance, it can make sense to say one sees the hand of God at work in overcoming a major obstacle but not to say one sees the hand of God at work in brushing the lint off one's suit.[2]

In a discussion of divine uniqueness we cannot pass by the orthodox Christian view of Jesus. For Christians there does seem to be a specific divine embodiment in Jesus. For orthodox Christianity God was in Christ, specifically embodied in Jesus. Of course, Jesus is God, the Son, not God, the Father or Holy Spirit, but still Jesus is specifically designated as God, for God is One. For orthodoxy, the doctrine of the Trinity does not eventuate in tritheism; monotheism remains intact.

Jesus, of course, as a man, is just another contingent human being and would appear in that fashion to non-Christians. Within orthodox Christianity itself, the problem of divine uniqueness seems to be solved by the embodiment of divinity in Jesus. This solution would apply whether we regarded God as necessary or contingent. Viewed as human, God as Son would be like other contingent objects in the world, but God as Father and as Holy Spirit would put God outside the category of other contingent objects. God, being one unity of Father, Son and Holy Spirit, would be a very special entity whether He was viewed as necessary or contingent.

Of course, viewed from the broad empiricist perspective taken in this study, we can only stipulate divine uniqueness to be centered in God but not manifested only in the specific embodiment of Jesus. It is obvious that divine uniqueness centered specifically in Jesus is available only to those in the Christian faith and only to those Christians who take a more or less orthodox theological view. Viewed empirically there is no justification for taking Jesus as the only human to embody divinity. Buddhism, for example, allows for multiple divine embodiment in persons, opening up again the ambiguities we spoke of earlier.

It is apparent that whatever or whoever God may be, His being cannot be that of thing, person, event or theoretical construct. The being of God consists in a unique and mysterious source of transcendent value experience. This transcendent value experience involves a relationship between us and God consisting of a felt, living, manifestation of goodness. It is true that God can appear as threatening or as an enemy too but, overall, our experience of God is value-positive. Thus, it seems plausible to regard God as being peculiarly unique though contingent rather than necessary.

The ordinary contingency of things and persons involves radical finitude which means that we and the things around us come into existence, exist for a time and then cease to exist altogether, at least as far as we can tell empirically. God's contingency would be special. While temporal, God seems to manifest Himself continuously in time. Since God manifests Himself contingently in the temporal world, we really don't know whether such manifestation will continue to occur in the future, though we may have faith and hope that it will.

Some encounter divinity in experiences of breath-taking and awe-inspiring wonder. Experiences of the aesthetically sublime frequently carry religious overtones as well. The vastness and overpowering aspects of nature and of our own insignificance, in comparison, lead many to feel that the overpowering aspect of divinity has been at least partially disclosed to them. Breath-taking sunsets, the vastness of the ocean and the immensity of the grand canyon lead some to feel that the overpowering aspect of God has been disclosed in these experiences. The aesthetically sublime can presumably be experienced without religious overtones, but when we are made almost painfully aware of our own smallness and finitude, it is hard to deny the religious overtones. The sublime also tends to introduce Otto's numinous aspect as well. It also tends to be mysterious and too great to really comprehend. In this kind of situation God tends to be wholly other and His transcendence can be overpowering.

On the other hand many disclosures of divinity are close, intimate and personal in a very special sense. God can be immanent in human consciousness in prayer and meditation manifesting the I-Thou encounter stressed by Buber. Many pray to God and disclose their most intimate fears and worries to Him with the full confidence that they are understood and loved. The closeness to God is well expressed in the parable of the lost sheep where each soul is precious and known to God.

Whether divine presence is really manifested or whether one is subject to individual or group hallucination is epistemically impossible to clearly determine. While hallucination and deception clearly can and do occur, the ubiquity in time and space of such phenomena makes some genuine divine impingement a real likelihood. Again, divine disclosure is contingent because the manifestations are empirical occurrences, lacking logical necessity. Since it is not logically necessary that God disclose himself at all and since such disclosures as occur are empirical, there is no basis to assume that divine uniqueness must rest on necessity.

Organized religions owe their metaphysical plausibility to the whole area of religious experience which is multifaceted and impressive. Most people, religious or not, may never report having a direct experience of divinity, but if the reports of such experiences were not as numerous and impressive as they are, organized religion could be explained away as a psychological crutch to aid us through a dangerous world.

Divinity, though contingent, manifests itself in very peculiar ways that are totally different from other contingencies and make it unique. The ways in which divine uniqueness is manifested are also ways which those who believe that God is necessary would accept. Their contention is that these divine disclosures could only be manifested by a necessary being, not a contingent one. We have seen that divine uniqueness is radically different from the type of uniqueness we are familiar with in ordinary contingent objects. It does not follow from this, however, that divine uniqueness is explicable only by appealing to necessity.

Contingency may have different facets. Contingent entities are not timeless, but while ordinary contingent objects come and go, it well may be that a contingent entity may eternally manifest itself through time. "Eternally" here does not mean "outside of time" but manifestation through time.

Divinity may be eternally manifested through time contingently, and for all we know, may be a feature of our cosmic epoch and not necessarily a feature of all possible worlds. Of course, traditional theism would reject outright such a view of the divine. It may seem implausible but it is hard to see how such a divinity is self-contradictory or religiously inadequate in any significant sense.

To insist that God must be eternal in an absolute sense and a creative factor behind all possible worlds is to desert our empirical base. We do not live in all possible worlds or outside our own cosmic epoch, and experience can tell us nothing about things that may be outside these parameters. Our religious life does not function outside of these parameters either. Worship and meditation occur in the world of our experience, throughout time and space. Empirically and contingently, divinity manifests unique and eternal aspects that no other kind of contingent entity possesses. The disclosures that occur are vast and impressive enough to be adequate to the religious life. James was wrong in thinking that divinity was *just* finite, without any further qualification. Contingent divinity is radically unique, and unlike anything else, but James's empirical insight that divinity is contingent still is sound. God is also a concrete entity, which makes His appearance in the world of time and change religiously significant.

If one requires God as an ultimate principle of explanation, one is probably doomed to eternal frustration and mystery. If God is required as a companion Thou in religious dialogue and worship, then life may take on new meaning and significance. The first requirement may demand a necessary being, but the second does not.

A unique though contingent divinity is as much as religious consciousness need ask for and as much as experience can justify.

NOTES

1. Rudolph Otto, *The Idea of the Holy* (New York: Galaxy Books, 1958).

2. If Whitehead is right, God is present in *all* situations acting as a "lure" for choice, but this does not change the fact that divine disclosure is empirically manifested more obviously in some situations than in others. Thus, God may be present metaphysically in everything, as pantheists and panentheists maintain, but empirically He is only manifested in situations where revelatory disclosure occurs.

CHAPTER XI
DIVINE CONTINGENCY, SO WHAT?

The question of whether God exists necessarily or contingently may still appear as a philosophical parlor game to some readers and, in a sense, it is. Philosophy is a highly abstract discipline. It is not meant to be immediately pragmatic. However, if we think that philosophy, due to its abstract nature, has no implications whatsoever for the lives of men in the world, we are sadly mistaken. The relationship between philosophy and practical affairs is somewhat analogous to the relationship between pure theoretical science and the manufacture of new items of technology. When the military and business communities build laboratories for the theoretical scientist, they would like immediate technological results. They find out, however, that in order to get the results they want they must let the theoretical scientist "play" games of pure theory in his laboratory. This procedure can be costly and frustrating for business and the military but it must be done because it is only through the "play" of pure theory that eventually the practical results will be achieved.

In a similar way, if we look behind the political revolutions and social concerns that drive masses of men, we will find a philosophical ideology of some kind at work, whether this is explicitly recognized or not. In an indirect sense, and given a long chain of causal influences, it appears that philosophy has much more pragmatic impact than we might suppose. World views involving basic attitudes about the world we confront drive the engines of practical life, though most of us are not explicitly aware of it.

Hegel and Marx were fully aware of this philosophical impact and developed their thought along lines that drew out the implications of philosophy for life in the world of political action. Whether they were accurate in their observations is not relevant at this stage of our study. That they were aware of these connections is sufficiently noteworthy in itself.

In the middle of the nineteenth century there was a man who went every morning, day after day, to the reading room of the British Museum and remained there until closing, reading and doing research of an abstract theoretical nature. If someone had noted this at the time and suggested that this ordinary man's plodding daily ritual would shake the world to its foundations in the next hundred years, that person would have been thought to be crazy.[1] Yet the man who visited the British Museum was Karl Marx and out of his research came his major work, *Das Kapital*. A consequence of this research was the formation of the world communist movement. We needn't labor the point that abstract theoretical ideas can eventually have dramatic impact on practical events.

The moral of this story as it applies to our study should be apparent. Theories about God and whether He exists necessarily or contingently are remote and abstract, but the views that historically have been taken on the question of God's nature have moved men to action. The connections between theory and practice may be long and devious but they are there.

The traditional Western Christian view of God is a product of both Jewish and Greek influences. Jehovah in many ways is modeled after a middle eastern potentate as Whitehead said. It is interesting to note that the god of Islam also appears as a domineering monarch. From the Greek backgound we get the static unchanging God analogous to a Platonic Form or to Aristotle's Prime Mover. While Christianity reflects both of these influences, the domineering potentate image has also been vigorously fought and resisted by various Christian believers and theologians.

The significant point concerning the domineering view of God is that Western society and its political institutions have operated from a world view that sees God as a supreme all-powerful ruler who must be supported against His enemies and ours. What emerges from this is a model of dominance and power which has made itself felt all through Western history.

Some would argue that this account is a gross misinterpretation of divine intentions as, indeed, it may be. The picture of God conveyed by Western societies down through history, however, is one of dominance, power and control. This theological world view has been at the base of Western political and military dominance for centuries.

I want to suggest that part of the philosophical and theological backup for a religiously domineering God was to see God as a necessary being. Here is where the Greek element, in particular, made its influence felt in Christian theology. Aristotle's prime mover as an eternal rational principle gets grafted onto the jealous Jewish god, Jehovah, and the graft that emerges at the high point of medieval Catholic culture is a picture of God as an all-powerful ruling potentate, who at the same time is an eternal rational principle, necessarily existing. This odd mix of Jewish and Greek influences continued to appear in Protestantism as well.

It would seem as though this Western mind-set of God as a supreme potentate and rational principle was a major factor leading to the unbridled technological dominance that the West achieved over the rest of the world by the nineteenth century. If this is so, the theoretical belief in an all-powerful dominating God who necessarily exists was a factor in the West's ability to develop a highly technological civilization before the East did.

The point is that an all-powerful domineering God gets things done and His followers are also to get things done. God has given us dominion over all the world and though we are to use that dominion wisely, like a shepherd tending his sheep, still we are entitled to remake the world to fit our purposes. The world is seen as a place where recalcitrant matter is to be coerced and shaped to answer our needs using ever more efficient technological tools.

Western technological dominance now threatens to engulf the world, for better or for worse. The West may have developed it most efficiently and exported it elsewhere, but all countries now want and need advanced industrial technology. Japan borrowed the Western mind-set after World War II and has refined and adapted it so skillfully to Japanese culture that Japanese technology and business are rapidly pushing towards world technological dominance. Korea is not far behind, and in the next century the Orient stands a good chance of beating the West at its own game.

The so-called Third World is rapidly gaining and developing technology with all the good and bad effects that accompany such technology. India, steeped historically in Hinduism with a profoundly different mind-set from the West, is becoming more Westernized all the time. Gandhi and passive non-violence were a natural legacy of a quietistic Hinduism, but Gandhi is dead and we find relatively little trace of his influence in the power politics of current India. She, like other countries, wants a strong military force with nuclear arms and eyes her neighbors with suspicion.

As for Russia, steeped in the mysticism of the Eastern church, she carried out her industrial revolution under the influence of Marxism, a thoroughly Western viewpoint. Except militarily, Russia is a Third World country, desperately in need of technological development.

The spreading of technology worldwide and what to do with its corresponding destructive effects on the environment will be the big story of the twenty-first century. What the outcome will be we do not know, but this issue will be a major part of the story in one way or another.

Returning to our study, it may seem odd to make belief in a necessarily existent all-powerful God the villain of the piece. To make it the only factor behind the changes we have witnessed would indeed be an error. Yet it seems plausible to see a God of power, a God who sends people out to convert the heathen as a God who *coerces* men in the world to meet His needs and expectations. Seeing God as necessary attempts a logical kind of coercion on us. The basic way a culture or a society perceives the world "deep down" is bound to affect the way men operate in the world. The domineering Western view of God and what He requires of men led not only to military conquest abroad but to the building of schools and hospitals in conquered territories. The Christian West took up the "white man's burden" to spread the blessings of Christian civilization worldwide. In Hindu India, schools and hospitals were not seen as that important. One was to accept the world and meditate on karma and the state of one's soul instead. Western dominance has spread but its effects are by no means all negative or destructive. We all now live in a world that can never realistically go back to the past even if we wanted to. Technology has produced many of our major problems and it will take an improved technology to correct them.

Abstract discussion of Anselm's ontological proof for the existence of God may seem light years away from what is unfolding in the world now. There is no simple causal chain leading from divine necessity to modern technological world dominance, but seeing God as logically necessary may be part of a complicated network of causal relations contributing to our current attitudes. Once God was declared to exist necessarily there was a closure and finality that presumably settled the God debate for all time. Before the ontological proof came to be accepted, an agnostic, atheist or simple unbeliever may have been a perverse sinner and heretic, but once the proof was in place, the non-believer was also irrational in refusing to see or understand the logic of the proof. In addition to lack of faith was added the sin of failing to follow the dictates of logic. Given the proof only "the fool" could really say, "There is no God."

In the area of religious faith and commitment, such closure of the issue is a disaster. All numinous wonder at the mystery of divine presence is removed and we have an open and shut case for God. This is not to say that

Anselm and others followed the apparent logic of their own approach. Most supporters of divine necessity were men of profoundly religious faith whose belief in God was always temporally and logically prior to their proof. For these men the so-called proof was always primarily a "testament of devotion" addressed to God in faith. By the time we reach the rationalism of Descartes, however, the proof is detached from the background of faith, and logic and reason are to carry the day alone.

In the post-Cartesian era the closure is in place and reason must justify religious faith to man. Reason became used in a broader sense than simple reference to the ontological proof. It included the proof but reason covered any rational attempt to prove God's existence. In the Eighteenth century the most widely used tool of reason was the argument from design. In the age of Enlightenment Christian faith continued, but for the enlightened modern man it must make sense, bowing before criteria set up by reason and logic. In addition to seeing God for centuries as an authoritarian ruler it becomes essential to add rational necessity to justify belief in Him. But wasn't the Enlightenment meant to free man from the authoritarian medievalism of the past? Yes, and in many ways it did but to those who desired that Christian conversion continue, reason was an added powerful tool to use in the coercive conversion process.

Not only is the appeal to authority a tool of dominance, the coercive epistemic force behind reason and science also becomes a tool of dominance. Who can resist what reason, faith and experience seem to demonstrate so clearly? Reason and science, when used to justify Christian faith, become an irresistible force. True, reason and science led many persons into skepticism and loss of faith, but culturally the West was forging an aggressive technological culture believing in unlimited progress under a divine injunction to go out and convert the heathen. By the nineteenth century the Bible and the flag had aggressively colonized Africa and Asia, not to mention South America. The philosophical high water mark of the process we have been describing was Hegel's grand synthesis, the triumph of the rational Christian world spirit.

Can Western technological expansion be blamed on the abstract doctrine of divine necessity? Not directly and immediately. Such a response would be much too crude and simplistic. What I am suggesting is that the belief in divine necessity was a strong link in the chain of circumstances leading to present technological dominance and its accompanying disregard for the larger environment.

"Necessity" is a coercive term and is meant to be. Logic is meant to coerce rational beings. The term is emotively loaded in this direction. I am not suggesting that it shouldn't be, but it is worth noting that it is. It is one thing to have this important function in logic but to carry it over as a coercive tool in politics or religion is something else. A main thrust of this whole study is that to use necessity as a coercive tool in religion is a profound misuse. Religiously the coercive mind-set rests on God, the potentate. Philosophically the coercive mind-set rests on divine necessity.

When we consider the major religions of the East the picture becomes quite different. There are coercive Eastern religions. Shintoism is an example, as is Islam in the middle East. But Hinduism and Buddhism, the major religions of the East, operate with quite a different perspective from that with which we have been dealing.

Hinduism, Buddhism and Taoism remained remarkably non-dogmatic and free from coercion compared with the West. The conversion mania seems to have been absent, at least until Western religious influences crept in. There were gurus under whom one could voluntarily study. Individual practice and meditation received considerably more emphasis than the group worship of Western religions. Indeed, the lack of emphasis on corporate worship may be a weakness in the Eastern approach. Belief in sound orthodox doctrine was far less important in these Eastern religions than in the West.

There is a major emphasis on mystical experience and on seeing the "tao" in all things. Quietism rather than coercion seems to characterize these Eastern traditions. Their approach to the environment is philosophically much sounder than ours. In theory, the environment is impregnated and immanent with divinity. The material world is not something to be molded to our will but something to to be appreciated and respected for divinity resides in all things. The Hindu-Buddhist world view is much more congenial with a divine gift-like contingency than it is with divine necessity.

Unfortunately, when one moves from theory to practice, theory consists more in what should be than in what is. Civilizations, both East and West, have engaged in environmental destruction and aggressive warfare. While the gap between the Ideal and the actual is wide in Christianity, it is equally wide in Buddhism and Hinduism. Religions the world over point us towards ideals to be realized, but as applied to civilizations, the ideals are corrupted or vanish altogether. Nevertheless, when looked at in terms of a philosophical world view, it would seem that Eastern religions are more environmentally coherent about man's place in the cosmos than are most Western views. There are, however, some native American views about man and the environment which are similar to those of Eastern religions.

Daniel Boorstin gives an interesting and revealing picture of the Chinese mentality viz a viz the West.[2] China, historically, has had as strong an ethnocentric viewpoint as civilizations in the West. Ancient China considered itself to be the center of the universe and superior to other cultures. But instead of aggressively marching out from their center to coerce the rest of the world, China, by persuasion, "...hoped to make 'the whole civilized world' into voluntary admirers of the one and only center of civilization."[3] Nothing suggested that China needed what other nations had. While Asians would be struck by the Western powers' ability to seize, the Chinese sought to impress by their ability to give products to the West. In the age of exploration by the West, China offered up treasures of the finest craftsmanship. As Boorstin so succinctly observes, "A state bringing tribute to China was not submitting to a conqueror. Rather it was acknowledging that China, by definition the *only* truly civilized state, was beyond the need of assistance."[4]

The Chinese believed that since China was the center of civlization the rest of the world would naturally come to China to seek what was better. China thus remained isolated and turned inward, admittedly complacent and self-righteous, backward in technology, convinced that it had nothing to learn from the inferior world around it. Why should China engage in expansion when everything worthwhile was already at home? Meanwhile the aggressive West, pushing outward from its center towards conquest, plundered China in the interest of God and business.

What is interesting to note is the profoundly different philosophical perspectives between the East and the West illustrated in this case, where both sides were equally sunk in their own kind of ethnocentricity. Of course, the situation has changed radically now. The East is now driven by Western technological mind-sets.

Looking at our present situation we see the Western, domineering, technological mind-set enveloping the entire planet, combined with an increasing number of ecological catastrophes produced by such mind-sets. Everybody wants the technology and everybody needs it. The destruction of the rain forests may produce jobs and economic benefits as it destroys the environment. This is an example of the kinds of paradoxes we face.

It is apparent that the environmental mess the entire world confronts is in large measure a result of the mind-set of planetary dominance. The Biblical insight that God gave man dominion over all the creatures of the earth became interpreted as dominance and control for exclusively human purposes rather than shepherding resources in the interest of *all* planetary life, including man.

Historically, the major religious traditions of the East have approached the world with a different mind-set. Deeply embedded in Hinduism, Buddhism and Taoism we see an attitude of "letting things be" rather than trying to dominate them and force them to submit to our wills. As we have seen, a quietistic nature mysticism characterizes each of these traditions. Again we must not fall into the trap of thinking the East is good and the West is bad and leave it at that. In actual practice, Eastern and Western societies have both degraded man and nature. Overall I am making the case that this Eastern theoretical view is preferable to the theoretical view of Western divine control whether this is seen in terms of dominance or shepherding. Even the shepherd is paternalistically superior to all else. This feature seems absent or subdued in the Eastern approach where we share with rather than shepherd over. But the world needs some of both. Eastern quietism may produce a more healthy and ethical attitude towards environmental conservation but it does not produce scientific and technological development, both of which are needed, no matter how often abused. It is no answer to wax romantic about Zen poetry and Chinese painting as the solution. In India, Hinduism existed for centuries with no questioning of the rigid caste system. Wives were being killed to be buried with their husbands and devout Hindus were worshipping cows while people starved to death. Concern with schools and hospitals was stimulated by Western influence, no matter how violently the concerns were carried out by Western empire building.

As to our concerns in this study, the issue of whether God is necessary or contingent is not remote and trivial as regards these social issues. Regarding God as a necessary being is part of a coercive domineering framework. It may not be a big step, but looking at divinity in a completely non-coercive way may contribute to changing our environmental attitudes. Regarding divinity as a contingent gift of experience would be a step in the right direction as well as being a profound disclosure of the divine nature.

We saw early in the chapter that deeply held philosophical and religious world views affect the course of pragmatic affairs though often quite unconsciously. Until a significant number of human beings the world over alter their basic thinking and attitudes about how man operates in the world we will continue to put band-aids on our environmental sores but we will not really do anything basic to save the environment.

The environmental movement has a dual thrust. One aspect of it comes out of the Western domineering world view, or at least operates within the context of that world view. In this aspect we see the environment in terms of how it affects *man*. This is the approach most familiar to us. We see our rivers, streams and oceans polluted and our forests destroyed and we wonder quite rightly how we will survive if we end up poisoning our own nests. This is a quite legitimate concern. What will happen to us if we go on as we are?

The other thrust of the environmental movement has the same concerns but asks its questions in a different framework. This thrust sees us, not as the domineering beings of the planet or even as its superior shepherds, but as co-inhabitors with other creatures and forms of life, who have prima facie rights, at least, to be taken into consideration. In this second aspect the world does not exist just to make us happy and satisfied. It exists as a place where we are to *share* resources with other forms of life. Humans cease to be the only creatures to have rights. The more thoughtful persons in the animal rights movement are making us aware of this aspect. Both aspects of environmentalism are legitimate concerns but I would suggest that the second aspect is more profoundly religious than the first and that until the second becomes more ingrained in human nature, we will only make patchwork attempts to shore up a worsening environment.

The implications of environmental concerns as they affect our study are now apparent. A contingent divinity does not rule and coerce the environment as a necessary being does but lures us to constantly create anew. A contingent divinity *shares* the world as gift, though surpassing the world in crucial ways. While the issue of necessity and contingency may not be raised, as such, the "letting be" aspect of classical Oriental mysticism seems far closer to divine contingency than to necessity. The "letting be" aspect is more pronounced in philosophical Taoism and Buddhism than in popular religion but it is there at the philosophical and religious base of these religions.

There is a long and involuted road from a necessary divine world ruler to rings of plastic choking pelicans to death. It is a long and involuted road from a contingent and persuasive divine being to nature preservation and population control but the connections and continuity of the roads are there. Basic philosophical and religious apprehensions of the world *do* shape the world we live in.

NOTES

1. An observation suggested by reading Isaiah Berlin, *Karl Marx: His Life and Environment* (London: Oxford University Press, 1963).

2. Daniel J. Boorstin, *The Discoverers* (New York: Vintage Books, 1985) Chapter 25.

3. *Ibid.*, p. 192.

4. *Ibid.*, pp. 192, 193.

CONCLUSION

For some readers my thesis is one they already accept and for them I hope the book has been helpful in bringing out aspects of ultimate contingency which they may not have noted. For those undecided at the outset and for those who still disagree with my thesis, I hope these pages will, at the very least, have provided food for thought.

Living in the world remains risky and tenuous no matter what philosophical or religious view we take. Viewed in purely philosophical terms, the issue of contingency and necessity may seem purely abstract and of no existential significance in the life of men. In religious terms however, we have seen how religious adequacy and divine uniqueness can be maintained with a contingent divinity.

Given a close look, the issue is a deeply important one. Philosophically, for many contemporary thinkers the issue is already "played out" in favor of ultimate contingency or at least the denial of ultimate metaphysical necessity. The rejection of foundationalism in epistemology plus the turning away from classical metaphysics has already resolved the issue for many in favor of contingency.

From a religious perspective, however, and in the view of a still vital philosophical and theological tradition, that the world could fail to be grounded in a necessary being and that the world could be "without why" entails a profoundly irreligious and unacceptable view. The thrust of the whole study is that ultimate contingency is not only coherent with religious faith and commitment, but that such contingency supports the actualities of religious faith far better than reliance on necessity.

In the last analysis, the appearance of anything at all in experience, including our own ability *to* experience, is gift-like and hence, contingent. In spite of the apparent unintelligibility of non-being or nothing at all, that there is anything whatsoever is remarkable and miraculous.

One might object that there always has to be something or other, or that the statement, "Something exists," is always necessarily true. This world and even this God would not have to be, but something would have to be, because sheer non-being is unintelligible.

In spite of apparent unintelligibility, sheer-non being is imaginable by some five-year olds even if they are in the picture imagining this themselves. To many deeply religious persons, the wonder that there is anything is felt as an overpowering and numinous gift. To them, not only is this world and divine grace a gift, not necessitated or required, but that any possible world or divinity should appear is an inexplicable gift. The world and divine grace, being gifts, would both be radically contingent because they appear gratis, not required or necessary. The marvel and awe at there being anything ever, is a profoundly religious attitude.

Most of the time we take the world and God for granted and go on about our business. To view the world and God with something of the wonder of a small child is deeply and profoundly spiritual. To be able to view the world in this way is the true gift of contingency, a gift which in the last analysis cannot be forced to disclose itself even by rigorous meditation practices. Our ability to view reality as a gift will have tremendous implications for our attitude towards the environment. Whether we will learn to live with the environment or continue to simply exploit it, is and likely will be, *the* underlying ethical issue of the next century.

If the book is helpful in furthering deeper sensitivity to the world around us it will have done as much or more than I could have hoped.

BIBLIOGRAPHY

Saint Anselm. *Basic Writings.* LaSalle, IL: Open Court Publishing Company, 1962.

Barth, Karl. *Church Dogmatics.* Edinburgh: T. and T. Clark, 1957.

——— . *Anselm: Fides quaerens intellectum; Anselm's proof of the Existence of God in the context of his Theological Scheme.* Richmond, VA: John Knox Press, 1960.

Berger, Peter L. *A Rumor of Angels.* Garden City, NY: Doubleday Anchor Books, 1970.

Berlin, Isaiah. *Karl Marx: His Life and Environment.* London: Oxford University Press, 1963.

Boorstin, Daniel. *The Discoverers.* New York: Vintage Books, 1985.

Buber, Martin. *I and Thou.* New York: Charles Scribner's Sons, 1958.

Cotton, J. Harry. *Royce on the Human Self.* Cambridge, MA: Harvard University Press, 1954.

Desan, Wilfred. *The Tragic Finale.* New York: Harper Torchbooks, 1960.

Dostoyevsky, Fyodor. *The Idiot.* New York: Modern Library, 1935.

Flew and Macintyre. *New Essays in Philosophical Theology.* London: SCM Press, 1955.

Fosdick, Harry Emerson. *As I See Religion.* New York: Harper & Brothers, 1932.

Hartshorne, Charles. *Man's Vision of God.* Hamden, CT: Archon Books, 1964.

——— . *The Logic of Perfection.* LaSalle, IL: Open Court Publishing

Company, 1962.

Heidegger, Martin. *Basic Writings*. New York: Harper and Row, 1977.

Hick, John. *An Interpretation of Religion*. New Haven: Yale University Press, 1989.

Hull, William I. *William Penn: A Topical Biography*. London: Oxford University Press, 1937.

Hume, David. *A Treatise on Human Nature*. Selby-Bigge edition, Oxford: Oxford University Press, 1967.

Huxley, Aldous. *The Doors of Perception*. New York and Evanston: Harper Colophon Books, 1963.

James, William. *Essays in Pragmatism*. New York: Hafner Publishing Company, 1949.

—————. *Essays in Radical Empiricism*. New York: Longmans, Green and Company, 1912.

—————. *The Varieties of Religious Experience*. New York: Longmans, Green and Company, 1935.

Kant, Immanuel. *Critique of Pure Reason*. Trans. Norman Kemp Smith. London: Macmillan Company, 1950.

Kierkegaard, Soren. *Philosophical Fragments*. Princeton, NJ: Princeton University Press, 1974.

Nietzsche, Friedrich. *Beyond Good and Evil*. Trans. Walter Kaufmann. New York: Vintage Books, 1966.

—————. *The Gay Science*. Trans. Walter Kaufmann. New York: Vintage Books, 1974.

—————. *The Portable Nietzsche*. Trans. Walter Kaufmann. New York: The Viking Press, 1968.

Noss, John B. *Man's Religions*. London: Macmillan, 1963.

Otto, Rudolf. *The Idea of the Holy*. New York: Oxford University Press, 1958.

Penney, Norman, ed. *The Journal of George Fox*. New York: E.P. Dutton and Co, 1924.

Platt, David. *Intimations of Divinity*. New York: Peter Lang Publishing. Co. Inc, 1989.

Reese, William L. and Freeman, Eugene, eds. *The Hartshorne Festschrift: Process and Divinity*. LaSalle IL: Open Court Publishing Company, 1964.

Rubenstein, Richard. *After Auschwitz*. Indianapolis: Bobbs-Merrill, 1966.

Sartre, Jean Paul. *Being and Nothingness*. Trans. Hazel Barnes. New York: Philosophical Library, 1956.

―――. *Nausea*. Trans. Lloyd Alexander. Norfolk, CT: New Directions, 1950.

Schürmann, Reiner. *Heidegger on Being and Acting: From Principles to Anarchy*. Bloomington, IN: Indiana University Press, 1987.

Smith, John E. *Themes in American Philosophy*. New York: Harper Torchbooks, 1970.

Watts, Alan. *Beyond Theology: The Art of Godmanship*. New York: Vintage Books, 1964.

Whitehead, Alfred North. *Process and Reality*. New York: Harper Torchbooks, 1960.

―――. *Religion in the Making*. New York: Meridian Books, 1960.

―――. *Science and the Modern World*. New York: Mentor Books, 1963.

Whitney, Janet. *John Woolman: American Quaker.* Boston: Little, Brown and Company, 1942.

Wiener, Philip P., ed. *Leibniz Selections.* New York: Charles Scribner's Sons, 1957.

Wild, John, ed. *Spinoza Selections.* New York: Charles Scribner's Sons, 1930.